The Sword of David

The Sword of David

The Israeli Air Force at War

Donald J. McCarthy Jr

Pen & Sword
AVIATION

First published in Great Britain in 2013 by
Pen & Sword Aviation
An imprint of
Pen & Sword Books Ltd
47 Church Street
Barnsley
South Yorkshire
S70 2AS

ISBN 978 1 78159 290 8

A CIP catalogue record for this book is
available from the British Library

Typeset in 10.5pt Palatino by Mac Style, Driffield, East Yorkshire
Printed and bound in India by Replika Press Pvt. Ltd.

Pen & Sword Books Ltd incorporates the imprints of Pen & Sword Archaeology, Atlas,
Aviation, Battleground, Discovery, Family History, History, Maritime, Military, Naval,
Politics, Railways, Select, Social History, Transport, True Crime, Pen & Sword Fiction,
Frontline Books, Leo Cooper, Praetorian Press, Remember When, Seaforth Publishing
and Wharncliffe.

For a complete list of Pen & Sword titles please contact
PEN & SWORD BOOKS LIMITED
47 Church Street, Barnsley, South Yorkshire, S70 2AS, England
E-mail: enquiries@pen-and-sword.co.uk
Website: www.pen-and-sword.co.uk

Contents

Dedication

To Lynda
My wife and best friend of over fifty years

Acknowledgements

It would have been impossible to complete this project without the help of many people who gave of their time and help. I wish to offer my thanks and sincere appreciation to those who have given to this project, many of whom started out as contacts and became good friends: Dave Hansen, Major Richard Kierbow USAF (Retd), Dave McNeil, Theo Elbert, Library Research, US Naval Aviation Museum, Major David Erff USAFR (Retd), Christine M. Pelka, Detective Sergeant Joseph D. DePasquale, Sergeant Roger Reed, Waterford Connecticut Police Department, Inspector Michael Hurley, State's Attorney Office.

I wish to offer a special thanks to the following friends who have opened up their photo collections to me; without them this project would never have been completed: Commander Peter Mersky USN (Retd), Ofer Zidon, Israel, Tsahi and Hagit Ben-Ami, Israel, Amos Dor, Israel, Sariel Stiller, Israel and R. Weiss.

Others to whom I'm truly indebted for their support with this project: Anne-Marie Lizarralde, Connecticut College Botany Department, for help in editing the manuscript, Tyler P. Petrini, photo selection/narratives, Leah N. Petrini, Nicolas I. Petrini, Natalie R. Petrini, Lieutenant Joseph A. San Juan Sr, Connecticut Army National Guard, (Retd) and Technical Sergeant Harvey O. Thorp, late Connecticut Air NG.

Introduction

In a speech given by Prime Minister Netanyahu of Israel during a ceremony honouring Israeli war dead he spoke about the future of Israel when he told the gathering, 'We extend one hand in peace to all our neighbours who wish for peace'. The Prime Minster continued, 'Our other hand grasps the Sword of David in order to defend our people against those who wish to kill us.'

The tip of the sword spoken of by Prime Minster Netanyahu is without doubt the combined armed forces of the State of Israel. At the very tip of the sword stands the Heyl Ha'Avir (Israeli Air Force) which today is called the Zroa Ha'Avir Ve'Halalal (Israeli Air and Space Force) (IASF). The air-to-air combat history of the IASF in the Middle East is legendary.

The best friend and strongest ally the United States has in the Middle East is undoubtedly the State of Israel. In 1947 the United Nations approved the partition of Palestine into two states, one Jewish and one Arab. The new State of Israel is located in the south-eastern edge of the Mediterranean where it borders Lebanon in the north, Syria and Jordan in the east and Egypt in the south-west. From its very inception Israel has been involved in major wars and has been further subjected to decades of violence.

Forged from many wars and countless attacks by its neighbours, the State of Israel has built and maintained one of the world's most powerful air forces. The Zroa Ha'Avir Ve'Halala (Israeli Air and Space Force) can claim more jet 'aces' than any other modern air force, among them being retired Israeli Air Force Reserve's Colonel Giora Even (Epstein), who is the world's leading jet ace with seventeen confirmed aerial victories. During the Yom Kippur War he shot down twelve Egyptian aircraft, eight of them in just twenty-six hours.

For more than thirty years the IASF security censors controlled the release of all information and photographs that showed IASF aircraft with unit markings. During the mid-1980s the restriction imposed by the censor was eased somewhat. *The Sword of David* features an outstanding collection of IASF aircraft photographs starting with the delta-winged fighters (Mirage and Nesher). Included in the collection are photos of Mirage IIICJ Nos. 158/159, each of which claimed thirteen combat aerial victories. The IASF was one of the first of America's allies to employ the F-4E Phantom in combat. While serving in the IASF the Phantom was used primarily as a strike fighter attacking ground targets. However, Phantom aircrews, while engaged in air base attack (ABA), battle field interdiction (BAI), suppression of enemy air defences (SEAD) and quick-reaction alert (QRA) missions were also credited officially with 116.5 aerial victories.

Many of the historic Phantoms of the IASF are presented on the pages that follow. Phantom 608 was the first IASF Phantom to be credited with an aerial victory. On 11 November 1969 No. 69 Squadron's Ehud Henkin and Achikar Eyal were the first IASF pilots to engage an Egyptian MiG-21 while on a combat air patrol (CAP) mission. In the ensuing air battle they downed the MiG with an AIM-9B Sidewinder air-to-air missile. *Kurnass* (Sledgehammer) No. 609 is the highest scoring F-4E Phantom II in the IASF with seven kills.

The air battles flown by the delta-winged Mirages and Neshers, and the Phantoms of the IASF against the Egyptians, Syrians, Jordanians, Libyans and even Russian and North Korean pilots are too numerous to count. The Mirages, Neshers and Phantoms of the IASF for the most part have flown their last combat missions in the simmering cauldron known as the Middle East. The IASF has rebuilt its air force around the American-designed and manufactured McDonnell-Douglas (now Boeing) F-15 Eagle and the General Dynamics (now Lockheed Martin) F-16 Fighting Falcon.

In 1976 Israel became the first American ally to receive the F-15 Eagle, known in the IASF as the Baz (Falcon). The Israelis were the first to take the Baz into combat when, on 27 June 1979, Lieutenant Colonel Moshe Melnik of the 'Double Tail' Squadron downed a Syrian MiG-21 with a Python-3 air-to-air missile. The F-15 flown that day was 663, nicknamed *Hamadlik* (Fire Igniter). Photos of this historic F-15 are featured along with photographs of all of the IASF F-15 Bazs credited with aerial victories while flying for various IASF squadrons. Another American-manufactured aircraft used by the IASF to maintain air supremacy is the F-16 Falcon. The F-16C/D models in the IASF are known as the Barak (Lightning) and have been deployed mainly as strike aircraft with the IASF. However, the Barak has proven itself as a dual-purpose aircraft. F-16s in Israeli service have claimed approximately forty-four Syrian aircraft of all types in air-to-air combat. Rafi Raz obtained the first kill on 28 April 1981 when he downed a Syrian Mi-8 helicopter in F-16 No. 112. What has to be the world's premier F-16 MiG killer is Barak No. 107 with six and a half kills. Colour photographs of both these historic F-16s appear in the pages of *The Sword of David*.

Since its very conception the Israeli Air and Space Force has fought overwhelming odds to protect the State of Israel from its many enemies in the Middle East. During its six major wars (1948 War of Independence, 1956 Sinai War, 1967 Six Day War, 1970 War of Attrition, 1973 Yom Kippur War and the 1982 Invasion of Southern Lebanon) the IASF has accumulated over 600 aerial victories. The record of aerial victories established by the IASF is truly impressive and nothing seems to capture the imagination like air-to-air combat. However, the primary mission of the IASF is not necessarily air-to-air combat but the destruction of enemy airfields with their aircraft, fuel and weapons storage areas, surface-to-air missile sites, anti-aircraft weapons, command and control centres, troop and armour concentration areas, supply depots, radar sites, POL (petrol, oil and lubricants) sites, communication centre and infrastructure facilities.

Often overlooked are the many unique and daring missions carried out by the IASF, such as the 7 June 1981 air strike against the Iraqi nuclear reactor. The jewel in the crown of the Iraqi nuclear programme was destroyed in a daring raid carried out by eight F-16s. Then, during the 1982 Invasion of Southern Lebanon the IASF destroyed over eighty-six Syrian MiGs without a single loss in air-to-air combat. More noteworthy, however, was the way in which the Syrian anti-aircraft and surface-to-air missile sites were totally destroyed. The combination of these two accomplishments sent the military leaders in the Kremlin into total panic. They had absolutely no answer as to how their top of the line fighters and other weapons systems had failed so miserably. On 1 October 1985 eight F-15 Bazs crossed the Mediterranean and, attacking in two waves, hit the PLO headquarters in Tunisia in retaliation for the killing of three Israelis in Larnaca, Cyprus.

In these pages there are many outstanding colour and black-and-white photographs of IASF aircraft that include all the F-15s that have claimed and been credited with air-to-air combat aerial victories as well as photographs of IASF F-16 Baraks credited with MiG kills, along with photos of all eight F-16s that took part in Operation OPERA.

Also included in are images of the two F-16 Baraks, Nos. 364 and 074 of the 'North Knights' and 'Valley' Squadrons, that shot down two Hezbollah Ababil unmanned air vehicles (UAVs), during the fighting in Lebanon in 2006. Impressive colour photographs of both aircraft, with new kill markings, depict them while they were on display at Ramat David Air Base on 24 April 2007.

This fantastic miscellany of IASF photographs and information regarding IASF missions is from the collections of Ofer Zidon, Tsahi Ben-Ami, Amos Dor and Anthony Hershko of Israel. Many of the colour photographs of IASF F-15s and F-16s in this book illustrate the dramatic new tail art on the F-15s and F-16s of today's IASF.

Also presented for the reader is a collection of photographs of IASF aircraft configured with the most modern air-to-air missiles, laser-, and satellite-guided munitions. Again these photographs are provided by Ofer Zidon, who is presently a photographer for the Israeli *Air Force Magazine*. It should be noted that all IASF photographs that appear in this book have been cleared by the Israeli Air and Space Force censor.

Some of the material contained in the narratives has been gleaned from a number of excellent literary sources in the field of military and aviation history. The author has quoted and paraphrased some material from the following: *Israeli F-4 Phantom II Aces* by Shlomo Aloni, (Osprey Publishing Limited, New York) and *Israeli F-15 Eagle Units in Combat*, by Shlomo Aloni, (Osprey Publishing Limited, New York).

I believe it was Thomas Jefferson who wrote 'A morsel of genuine history is a thing so rare as to be always valuable'. What I've attempted to do in this book is to present to the reader a morsel of genuine aviation history in both words and photographs.

Donald J. McCarthy Jr
Detective Commander (Retd)
Waterford Police Department
Waterford
Connecticut
2008

Chapter One

The Early Years and Beyond

The Chel Ha'Avir (Israeli Defence Force/Air Force) was formed officially on 28 May 1948, shortly after Israel declared statehood. Most of the fighter pilots of the newly-formed IDF/AF were volunteers who had fought in the Second World War. The fledgling Chel Ha'Avir(Israeli Defence Force/Air Force (IDF/AF) was comprised mostly of obsolescent Second World War aircraft, such as the Supermarine Spitfire (approximately sixty-two) and the Czechoslovak-built Messerschmitt (Bf109) Avia S-199. The Israeli Defence Force/Air Force initiated combat operations on 29 May 1948 when it launched four newly-arrived S-199s (Sakeen or Knife) flown by Lou Lenart, Modi Alone, Ezer Weizman and Eddie Cohen against Egyptian Forces near Isdud in the northern part of the Gaza district. The attack was not without cost to the Israelis, who lost two of their S-199s and, more importantly to the Israelis, the loss of the South African-born Messerschmitt pilot Eddie Cohen who was shot down and listed as killed in action. Eddie Cohen thus became the first person to be listed on the Roll of Honour for the Israeli Defence Force/Air Force.

The first aerial combat victories claimed by the Chel Ha'Avir came on 3 June 1948 when Modi Alon, flying an Avia S-199 (No. D.112) downed two converted Egyptian DC-3s. The DC-3s had just completed a bombing raid on Tel Aviv when Alon engaged them with cannon-fire, sending both to the desert floor. As the war continued the IDF/AF began to demonstrate its ability to gain air superiority over the combined Arab air forces. This was truly illustrated on 8 June 1948 when, for the first time, an Israeli aircraft flown by Gideon Lichtaman engaged and downed an Egyptian Spitfire in a dogfight.

By the end of the war in 1949 the IDF/AF had established total air supremacy in the skies over Israel with the infusion of new weapons systems like the Boeing B-17, de Havilland Mosquito, and P-51 Mustang. However, even with more and newer weapons, it has always been the men and woman of the IDF/AF who have made the difference in battle.

During the 1950s the French became the major supplier of aircraft to the Chel Ha'Avir. The IDF/AF entered the jet age during that decade, obtaining from the French the Dassault Mystère IV and Dassault Ouragan (1955–71), which flew alongside the British Gloster Meteor (1953–70). Super Mystère B-2s arrived in 1958, followed by one of the most famous of all French fighters deployed by the IDF/AF, the Dassault Mirage IIIC.

War would again come to the Middle East during 1956 with Egypt's Gamel Abdel Nasser's decision on 26 July 1956 to nationalize the Suez Canal, thus denying Israeli shipping the use of the Straits of Tiran. On 29 October 1956 Nasser's decision would bring Egypt into direct conflict with Britain, France and Israel. At the end of the Suez Crisis, also known as the Tripartite Aggression, the Straits of Tiran were re-opened to Israeli shipping.

The relationship between Israel and its major weapons supplier, France, would become strained during the late 1950s. Just prior to the Six Day War the relationship deteriorated to the point that France declared, and imposed, a total weapons embargo on the Israelis. As a result of the arms embargo the Israelis sought help from the United States to fill the void in modern weapons.

Throughout the 1960s, 1970s, 1980s, and even into the present day (2013) the Middle East was either in a state of war or on the verge of major military confrontation between Israel and the Arab states.

On 5 June 1967 the Middle East erupted into war, the Six Day War, when the Israelis launched pre-emptive airstrikes against the air forces of Egypt, Syria and Jordan. After just six days the IDF/AF claimed the destruction of over 452 enemy aircraft, forty-nine of which were claimed as aerial combat victories.

As strange as it may seem, prior to the Six Day War the IDF/AF did not possess a single air combat 'ace'. However, during the Six Day War Israel's first true ace was to step forward and claim that title. Brigadier General Giora Rom would not only be declared the IDF/AF's first true ace, he would also become the first Mirage IIICJ (Shahak) ace.

During the early stages (5 June 1967) of the Six Day War, Giora Rom was sitting on alert at Tel Nof Air Base when his flight was scrambled to intercept a flight of Egyptian MiG-21s that were about to attack a flight of IDF/AF strike aircraft. In the ensuing air battle Rom and his wingman, Eitan Karmi, would claim the destruction of two Egyptian MiG-21s. Rom would be credited with the downing of a Syrian MiG-21 during the afternoon of 5 June 1967. On 7 June 1967 Rom would again engage Egyptian MiGs. His flight of three Shahak delta-winged fighters had been sent to intercept a flight of MiG-17s in the area of Bir Gifgafa. When all

was said and done, the Israeli Air Force had its first true ace. Rom had engaged two of the MiG-17s, sending both to the desert floor in flames.

On 30 July 1970 the Middle East again boiled over into war, the War of Attrition, when the IDF/AF engaged in a large-scale air battle. The IDF/AF had set and executed an ambush (Operation RIMON 20) which brought them into direct combat with a larger flight of Egyptian MiG-21s flown by Russian pilots. The IDF/AF ambush resulted in the destruction of five Russian-piloted MiGs without a single Israeli aircraft being damaged.

In October 1973 the Arab states, led by Egypt and Syria, launched a simultaneous attack across the Suez Canal and against the strategic Golan Heights to open the Yom Kippur War. The IDF/AF played a major role during the war and again demonstrated that the skies of the Middle East were controlled by the Israeli Air Force. A total of 334 Egyptian and Syrian aircraft were shot down in air-to-air combat during the Yom Kippur War. Shortly after the war the United States became Israel's principal supplier of front-line combat aircraft. The first American front-line combat aircraft to enter service with the IDF/AF were the F-4E Phantom II and A-4 Skyhawk. These two proven combat veterans would be followed by the American designed and built F-15 Eagle, F-16 Fighting Falcon and E-2 Hawkeye.

For over sixty-three years the state of Israel has been under constant attack by major armies and terrorist groups of the Middle East. Yet the Israeli Defence Forces have met all challenges forced upon them, and have always prevailed. The Israeli Defence Force/Air Force in co-operation with other branches of its military has carried out a number of military operations that have become legendary.

Beyond The Major Wars

Time and space do not allow for a complete description of the full impact of the many classified missions conducted over the years by the Israeli Defence Forces. However, a number of these combat operations carried out by the IDF helped the Israelis to maintain their combat edge in the Middle East.

Most of the world was stunned when word of the attack, Operation OPERA (also known as Operation BABYLON), by Israel on the Iraqi nuclear reactor on 7 June 1981 leaked out. How the Israelis were able to destroy Saddam Hussein's nuclear programme in a single air strike has been well documented over the years. However, there are some lesser-known operations, most of which are still classified by the Israelis, for example:

On 26 September 1969, Israeli helicopters carrying paratroopers carried out a successful raid (Operation ROOSTER 53) to capture an advanced Soviet P-12 radar installation in Egypt near Suez, and returned the entire site to Israel without a single loss of its troops or equipment.

During the War of Attrition, 7 January–13 April 1970, Israeli Phantoms conducted air strikes into the very heartland of Egypt against major military targets. The missions were carried out under the code name Operation PRIHA (Blossom).

Operation RIMON 20 was a carefully orchestrated ambush planned to lure Russian pilots flying Egyptian MiGs into aerial combat. The ambush was the result of a Russian flown MiG attacking and damaging an Israeli A-4 with an air-to-air missile. The operation, carried out on 30 July 1970, resulted in the destruction of five Egyptian Air Force (EAF) MiGs without a single loss to the Israelis.

During 1982 hostilities broke out once more in the Middle East between Israelis and the Palestinian Liberation Organization (PLO). On 6 June 1982 the Israeli Defence Forces launched Operation PEACE FOR GALILEE. Once again it was the overwhelming superiority in weapons that dictated the outcome of the operation. The Israeli Defence Force/Air Force with its great technological advantage was able to destroy the Syrian surface-to-air missile batteries in the Beqaa Valley. As a result of the Israeli military victory the PLO was expelled from Lebanon.

After their expulsion from Lebanon in 1982 the PLO relocated their headquarters in Hammam al-Shatt in Tunisia. On 25 September 1985 an elite section of the PLO, known as Force 17, attacked and killed three Israeli civilians holidaying on a yacht off the coast of Cyprus.

In response to the unprovoked murder of the three Israeli civilians the IDF/AF launched Operation REGEL ETZ (WOODEN LEG). Eight heavily-armed F-15s took off from Tel Nof Air Base in Israel, their destination the Palestine Liberation Organization headquarters in Tunisia. Upon completing the 1,280-mile flight to their targets the bomb-laden F-15s laid waste to the PLO headquarters, killing many members of the Force 17 terrorist group.

On 6 September 2007 Israeli aircraft conducted Operation ORCHARD. The operation was yet another precision air strike. This time the target was the Syrian and North Korean nuclear site under construction in the Deir ez-Zoe region. Under the cover of darkness F-15Is (Ra'am) and F-16Is (Sufa) aircraft took off from Hatzerim Air Base. At least eight aircraft armed with AGM-45 Maverick air-to-ground missiles and 500lb bombs were involved in the attack. Initial reports indicated that the

No. 69 Squadron aircraft had turned the nuclear site into a big hole in the desert floor.

Information for Operation ORCHARD is alleged to have come from an Iranian general, Ali Reza Asgari, who disappeared sometime in February 2007 and, as mentioned, may have been the source of the intelligence which led to the Syrian nuclear site attack.

During January and February 2009 the Israelis again demonstrated their ability to reach out into the unknown and attack their enemies in their own lair. Acting on creditable intelligence, the IASF displayed great tenacity and endurance when they conducted air strikes in Sudan against two convoys of trucks loaded with weapons headed for Egypt. The convoys were attempting to smuggle weapons into the Gaza Strip. As a direct result of the raid a total of seventeen trucks and thirty-nine smugglers were destroyed or killed.

The combat narratives represented in 'Beyond the Major Wars' are some of the most famous – or infamous depending on one's perspective – that have taken place over the years in the Middle East. It is most fortunate for Israelis, however, that the IASF has emerged from each conflict with total command of the skies over their country.

The enduring legacy of the Israeli Air and Space Force (IASF) over its enemies is not its overwhelming superiority in weapons technology or its enemies being technically inept. It is the personal qualities of its people, for man will always be the final power in war. The Israelis have produced many pilots who have during air combat operation validated the warfare doctrine of the General Staff, such as the world's leading jet ace, Giora Epstein, with seventeen confirmed kills.

Chapter Two

Shaping the Sword of David

Six Day War: 5–10 June 1967

During May 1967 the tension in the Middle East was again being brought to boiling point by the Arab countries. For a number of weeks, beginning around 15 May 1967, Israeli intelligence had been monitoring the military activities of the Egyptians, Syrians and Jordanians. The Israelis had detected the massing of troops, tanks, and artillery for an invasion into the very heart of Israel. The combined armed forces of Egypt, Syria and Jordan were to be augmented with troops and equipment from other Arab countries. Faced with the overwhelming military advantage of the joint Arab armies, the government of Israel decided to launch a pre-emptive air strike.

During the early morning hours of 5 June 1967 the Heyl Ha'Avir (IAF) executed Operation FOCUS, a pre-designed air operation to attack airfields in Egypt, Syria and Jordan in the hopes of delivering a devastating and crippling blow to the combined air forces of Egypt, Syria, and Jordan. At approximately 0700 hours on 5 June 1967 waves of Israeli aircraft launched from air bases throughout the country heading for Egypt. Between 0714 and 0855 hours eleven airfields, including the main air base at Bir Gifgafa in the Sinai, were attacked. During the first wave over 189 Egyptian aircraft were destroyed on the ground. A very small number of Egyptian aircraft were able to get airborne during the initial attack. In challenging the strike flights of the Israelis, the Egyptian MiGs

were quickly engaged by Mirage III delta-winged fighters of Nos. 101/103 Squadrons. In the one-sided air battle that took place eight Egyptian aircraft were sent flaming to the ground. In the first hours of the battle six Egyptian air bases were destroyed, along with sixteen radar sites.

With the destruction of most of the Egyptian Air Force, the Israelis turned their attention to Jordanian airfields in Amman and Mafrak as well as the Syrian airfields in Damascus, Damir and Sheikel. Even the H-3 airfield in Iraq near the Syrian border was hit by the Israelis.

Within approximately three hours on the first day the Israelis had established complete air supremacy over the battlefield. With no air threats to deal with, the air force was able to direct all its air assets to supporting the ground troops.

After six days of fighting Israel claimed to have destroyed a total of 452 Arab aircraft, of which forty-nine were aerial combat victories. The Six Day War had ended in a resounding defeat for the Arabs, but history has shown that the battle was not over.

War of Attrition 1969–1970

As early as July 1967 the Arab countries (Egypt, Syria and Jordan) initiated the War of Attrition against the State of Israel. Having been re-supplied by the Russians who, coincidentally, were attempting to reverse the poor showing of their equipment during the Six

Day War, the Egyptians launched massive artillery attacks along the Suez Canal in the hope of disrupting the Israelis' attempts to consolidate their gains from the Six Day War.

Lacking the artillery to go gun to gun with the Egyptians along the canal, the Israelis called once again on their air force to exact heavy losses on the Egyptians in both equipment and ground forces.

During the height of the battle the Israelis rushed into service newly acquired American A-4 Skyhawks and F-4E Phantoms. Not only were the Phantoms able to attack air defences along the Suez Canal they were able to hit strategic radar and communications stations, SA-2 missile batteries, anti-aircraft sites, army camps, supply bases and command headquarters located deep in Egyptian territory.

During July 1970 tensions peaked when an Egyptian MiG flown by a Russian pilot fired an air-to-air missile at an Israeli A-4. Though heavily damaged, the A-4 was able to make it safely home. It was known by the Israelis that Russian pilots were flying Egyptian MiGs prior to the attack on the A-4. For the most part the Russian pilots had restricted their mission to air base defence. With this overt hostile act by the Russians the Israelis launched operation RIMON 20.

On 30 July 1970 the operation was set in motion, designed to lure Russian pilots into attacking what they would believe were Israeli reconnaissance aircraft. What waited for the unsuspecting Russian pilots, who were eager to engage the Israeli pilots in air-to-air combat, were flights of Mirage IIIs and F-4E Phantoms configured for air-to-air combat. Even more ominous for the unsuspecting Russian pilots was who was flying the delta-winged Mirages and Phantoms. All the pilots were experienced combat pilots who had been credited with many MiG kills between them.

As hoped, the Russians took the bait, hook line and sinker, taking off in their Egyptian-marked MiGs. When it was all over there were five MiGs burning in the desert with not a single Israeli loss. The Russians never again ventured out to engage the Mirages and Phantoms of the Israeli Air Force.

During the War of Attrition the armed forces of Israel undertook a number of unique and daring operations: notably Operation ROOSTER 53 on 26 September 1969. Under cover of darkness SA-321 Super Frelon (Tzir'a) and Sikorsky CH-53 Sea Stallion (Yasur) helicopters carrying troops crossed into Egypt near Suez. Their mission was right out of a spy novel: enter Egypt undetected, capture an advanced Soviet P-12 radar site, hook the radar and support vans to the CH-53s and, again undetected, fly the P-12 radar equipment back to Israel. The mission was carried out without a single loss.

Operation PRIHA (Blossom) was undertaken from 7 January to 13 April 1970 as a series of relentless and concentrated air strikes against military targets deep in Egypt. The strike flights not only had to deal with Russian supplied surface-to-air missiles, but Egyptian MiGs. The Israelis lost approximately fifteen aircraft, mostly to surface-to-air missiles and anti-aircraft weapons. However, in air-to-air combat, which at times was like an old wild west gunfight, the Israelis claimed 111 aerial victories over Arab MiGs, for the loss of only four aircraft.

Yom Kippur War 6–26 October 1973

Having been re-armed by the Soviets with their most modern military hardware, the Arab states were ready to avenge the mauling their combined armed forces had suffered as a result of the Six Day War and the War of Attrition. Egypt, Syria and nine other Arab countries, augmented with troops, tanks, artillery and aircraft of at least four non-Middle Eastern nations, stood on the verge of attacking the State of Israel. To put it in perspective, the size of the Arab armies set to attack Israel has been described as being the equivalent of the total forces of NATO in Europe being unleashed on Israel.

On 6 October 1973, the holiest day in the Jewish calendar, Yom Kippur (Day of Atonement), the onslaught was set in motion. Along the Suez Canal (Bar Lev Line) 80,000 Egyptian troops supported by tanks, over 2,000 artillery pieces and aircraft attacked a small Israeli force, numbering approximately 436 defenders. The Bar Lev Line is situated along the eastern bank of the Suez Canal. In less than an hour, during the first moments of the Yom Kippur War, the Egyptians unleashed over 10,500 artillery shells. On the Golan Heights approximately 180 Israeli tanks were set upon by over 1,400 Syrian tanks supported by ground troops. The Egyptian Air Force, re-stocked with Russian MiGs, launched 200 aircraft in a simultaneous attack on three air bases, Hawk missile batteries and command and control units of the Israelis. The air bases at Refidim and Bir Tamada were temporarily put out of action.

The Israelis were held in a totally defensive posture for the first two to three days of the war. It wasn't until Israel had completely mobilized its reserves that it was able eventually to repulse the invaders and carry the war deep into the very heart of Egypt. Israeli ground forces, once on the offensive and supported by the Israeli Air Force, came within sixty-three miles of Cairo, and twenty-five miles of Damascus, before the advance was halted when a ceasefire was declared.

The Yom Kippur War ended on 25 October 1973 with the total encirclement of the Egyptian Third Army on the Egyptian side of the Suez Canal and with Israeli tanks and troops well on their way to Cairo and Damascus.

The war, as with all wars, was extremely costly to both sides. The Egyptians and Syrians have never disclosed their losses and thus ascertaining reliable figures is difficult. Estimated losses for the Arab states have been as low as 8,000 killed with 18,000 wounded. Several sources place the casualty list as high as 16,000 killed with over 35,000 wounded.

Arab tank losses were over 2,250 with over 400 tanks in good working order falling into the hands of the Israelis. Aircraft losses sustained by the combined Arab countries have been estimated as high as 514 with 334 aircraft lost in air-to-air combat with the Israeli Air Force.

Like the Arab states it is difficult to obtain precise figures as to Israelis killed in action. Again based on some estimations, Israeli killed and wounded have been set at approximately 2,500 killed with an additional 7,500 to 8,000 wounded. Approximately 400 tanks were put out of action. However, many of the tanks were returned to service even during the war. The Israeli Air Force is reported to have lost 102 aircraft; thirty-two F-4Es, fifty-three A-4s, eleven Mirages and six Super Mystères. Most of the aircraft were lost to the advanced Russian weapons (medium range SA-6 mobile surface-to-air batteries, self-propelled anti-aircraft weapons (SPAAG), and SA-7 man-portable air defence systems (MANPADS) during the first three days of the war.

During the Six Day War (1967), the War of Attrition (1970) and the Yom Kippur War (1973) the French-built Dassault Mirage III CJ was the principal air defence fighter of the IASF. The Shahak, meaning Sky Blazer, ruled the skies of the Middle East. During the Six Day War sixty enemy aircraft were claimed with the loss of only twelve IASF aircraft; in the War of Attrition 111 enemy claimed for the loss of four IASF aircraft and in the Yom Kippur War 277 for the loss of five IASF aircraft.

The Mirage III CJ claimed its first aerial victory on 14 July 1966 when Captain Yoram Agmon downed a Syrian MiG-21 with cannon-fire. The Mirage flown by Captain Agmon that day was No. 159. This particular Mirage would go on to claim a total of thirteen Syrian and Egyptian aircraft during its career with the IASF.

1982 Lebanon War – (MOLE CRICKET 19)

The 1982 Lebanon War was preceded by a massive build-up of the Syrian surface-to-air missile sites in the Beqaa Valley. The installation of the overlapping surface-to-air missile network was, of course, carried out by the Soviet Union. The Syrians were not only provided with the necessary hardware but also Soviet technicians and troops to help operate the system.

To counter the Syrian build up in the Beqaa Valley the Israeli Air Force launched Operation MOLE CRICKET 19.

On 9 June 1982 Israeli Air Force A-4 Ahit (Skyhawks), F-4E Kurnass (Phantoms) and F-16 (Falcons) attack aircraft were tasked with crippling the Syrian air defence systems in the valley. During the operation AH-1 Cobra helicopters were deployed to carry out air strikes against Syrian armoured vehicles, including Russian T-72 tanks.

Israeli Air Force F-15s and F-16s were launched to carry out combat air patrol (CAP) missions to protect Israeli strike fighters. During the CAP missions Israeli pilots shot down over eighty Syrian MiGs without losing a single aircraft in air-to-air combat.

Chapter Three

Elite Combat Aircraft of the Israeli Air and Space Force

Dassault Mirage IIICJ (Shahak)

Israel Aircraft Industries Nesher

It can be argued that the Dassault Mirage III and IAI Nesher would not fall into the category of post-Vietnam aircraft. However, both the Mirage III and Nesher played pivotal roles in the combat history of the Israeli Air and Space Force in air-to-air combat in the Middle East. The French-built Dassault Mirage IIICJ is undoubtedly the most famous of the IASF delta-winged fighters and was used by Israel from 7 April 1962 to 1982/83 as an air superiority fighter. The Mirage was obtained to counter the Russian-supplied MiG-21s then entering service with Arab countries. During three wars (Six Day War, War of Attrition and Yom Kippur War) and countless engagements the Mirage, also known by the nickname Shahak, destroyed in aerial combat approximately 282.5 enemy aircraft of all kinds. The first IASF Mirage kill took place on 14 July 1966 (Bastille Day) when Captain Yoram Agmon shot down a Syrian MiG-21. The aircraft flown during this confrontation was No. 159. This historic Israeli Shahak would during its service life be credited with thirteen aerial victories.

The second most significant delta-winged fighter to enter service with the IASF is the Israeli Aircraft Industries (IAI) Nesher. The

No. 745 is yet another unique Mirage III. Note the rare kill combination on the nose of the aircraft. Depicted are two Iraqi kill markings along with one Lebanese Hunter. Seated in the foreground is the IDF/AF Chief of Staff (1964–68) the late Prime Minister Yitzhak Rabin. On 4 November 1995 Yitzhak Rabin was assassinated by a radical right-wing orthodox Jew, Yigal Amid. (O. Zidon Collection)

Nesher No. 561 was credited with twelve aerial combat victories while deployed with the Hornet and First Fighter Squadrons. This photograph was taken in 1974 during a visit by the Israeli parliament's foreign and security committee to the Israeli Air Force. The man in uniform in the middle is General Beni Peled, IAF Commander. On his right is Menachem Begin who became Israel's prime minister (1977–83). Far left with back to camera is Yitzchak Shamir who succeeded Begin in the prime minister's office. The others are members of the committee. (O. Zidon Collection)

French government had been the major weapons supplier to Israel for many years. On or about 3 June 1967, however, the French government imposed a weapons embargo on Israel. The refusal of France to fulfill its contractual obligations to supply Mirage fighters, already paid for, forced the Israelis to come up with a replacement for the Mirage.

Much has been written over the years about the Israeli-built Nesher and how it came to be. The most popular to this day are the cloak-and dagger stories dealing with the plans for the French-designed Dassault Mirage being stolen in an ultra-secret operation by the Israeli intelligence service, Mossad. However, there are claims that Israel received fifty Dassault Mirage Vs in crates from the French Air Force.

Yet another story that has circulated over the years concerns Marcel Dassault who, prior to the Second World War, was Marcel Bloch, of Jewish extraction. During the war he was interned in concentration camps and only at the last minute was able to escape death at Auschwitz. The story continues that it was Dassault himself who gave the blueprints of the Mirage V to Israel. In any event the Israelis did obtain blueprints for the Mirage and were able to build the Nesher and Kfir delta-

Specifications: (Mirage IIICJ Shahak)

Crew: one
Length: 53 feet 6 inches
Wingspan: 28 feet 10 inches
Height: 12 feet
Empty weight: 14,880 pounds
Power plant: Atar 9B (9C) 4,280kg dry thrust; 6,400kg with afterburner
Maximum speed: Mach 1.4 at sea level; Mach 2.2 at altitude
Service ceiling: 59,000 feet
Rate of climb: 16,400 feet/minute
Guns: two 30-mm cannon
Missile: Two short range IR guided AAMs (Shafrir 1 and 2); one medium range Radar guided AAM Matra R.530

winged fighters. As the Neshers aged the jets were written off by the Israelis. Approximately sixty were sold and exported to Argentina where they were renamed Dagger by the Argentinians. The vast majority of the aircraft were deployed to the southern naval base at Rio Grande, Tierra del Fuego.

Like the Mirage III, the Nesher (Vulture) was a highly successful fighter while deployed by the IASF. The Nesher squadrons claimed, and were credited with, over 100 kills during the Yom Kippur War in 1973.

Specifications: (IAI Nesher – Vulture)

Crew: one
Length: 51 feet 5 inches
Wingspan: 374.58 square feet
Height: 14.76 feet
Empty weight: 14,551 pounds
Takeoff weight: 30,203 pounds
Power plant: 1 x SNECMA Atar C Turbojet; Military Power 4,250kg / 6,000kg with afterburner
Maximum speed: Mach 2.2
Guns: 2 x 30mm cannon

To date the world's leading jet ace is Giora Epstein of the Israeli Air Force, who has been credited with seventeen aerial combat victories. Epstein scored twelve of his victories while flying Nesher No. 561. Epstein used a combination of weapon systems in downing the enemy MiGs. He successfully used cannon-fire to bring down seven, two fell victim to the heat seeking AIM-9D Sidewinder and three to the Shafrir 2 air-to-air missile. (P. Mersky Collection)

IAI Kfir C.2 (Lion Cub)

Israeli Aerospace Industry

The Israeli Aerospace Industry Kfir C.2 was designed and built as a multi-role, delta-winged fighter. The Kfir features all Israeli avionics and is powered by an Israeli-made version of the General Electric J-79 turbojet engine which enables it to reach a maximum speed of 1,516mph (1,317 knots).

The birth of the Israeli Lion Cub is truly an amazing story. As a result of the Six Day War, the Israeli Air Force found itself in need of a new multi-role fighter to counter the newer advanced aircraft being supplied to its enemies by the Russians. The Six Day War also depleted many of the air assets of the IAF. Due to the circumstances in which the IAF found itself, an order for fifty Mirage multi-role day fighters was placed with the French government. The fifty aircraft were bought and paid for and ready for delivery to the

Israelis when President Charles De Gaulle placed an arms embargo on the sale of arms to Israel.

Finding itself literally between a rock and a hard place the Jewish state ordered agents of Mossad, one of Israel's most ultra-secret intelligence agencies, into action. During the covert operations conducted by Mossad the agency was able to acquire plans for the

The IAI Kfir No. 874 is the only Kfir to claim an aerial combat victory during its service life. On 27 July 1979 Israeli F-15s and Kfir delta-winged fighters were flying escort for attacking Israeli fighter bombers in the area of Lake Kar'um and the port of Sidon when they engaged a flight of five Syrian MiG-21s. It was during this air battle that Captain S. scored the first and only kill ever credited to a Kfir. Coincidentally, it was Captain S's first kill. Kfir 874 is depicted in this photograph in the markings of the 'First Fighter' squadron. Now retired from active service the historic aircraft sits in the hot sun at the ISAF Museum, Beersheba-Hatzerim, Israel.

Specifications: Kfir C.2 (Lion Cub)

Crew: one
Length: 51 feet 4 ¼ inches
Wingspan: 26 feet 11 ½ inches
Height: 14 feet 11 ¼ inches
Empty weight: 16,060 pounds
Load weight: 25,580 pounds, with two drop tanks and two AAMs
Maximum takeoff weight: 35,715 pounds
Power plant: 1 x 1A1 Bedeb-built General Electric J-79-J1E turbojet
Maximum speed: 1,516mph (1,317 knots)
Combat radius: 415 nautical miles (477 miles)
Rate of climb: 45,950 feet/minute
Guns: 2 x Rafael-built 30mm DEFA 553 cannon; 140 rounds per gun
Rockets: assortment of unguided air-to-ground rockets
Missile: 2 x AIM-9 Sidewinder or Shafrir or Python series AAM; 2 AGM-Maverick ASMs
Bombs: assortment of payloads up to 12,730lb on nine external hardpoints

Mirage III which were used in the design of the Kfir. Israel has never given any details of how they acquired an estimated 150,000 documents and drawings which covered every aspect of the design of the Kfir.

The Kfir C.2 entered service with Israel's No. 101 Squadron, the First Fighter squadron, during 1975 but didn't claim its first aerial combat victory until 27 July 1971. The pilot, identified only as Captain S., was flying at 400 knots at approximately 12,000 feet when he launched an air-to-air missile which detonated next to a Syrian MiG-21. The pilot of the enemy MiG was seen to bale out as the MiG went down, trailing a plume of smoke.

In the mid-1980s combat service for the Kfir was coming to an end with the addition of the F-4E Kurnass, F-15 Baz and the F-16

Netz to the inventory. The Kfir did, however, participate in the Israeli invasion of Southern Lebanon in 1982 (Operation PEACE FOR GALILEE).

Douglas A-4 Skyhawk (Ahit – Eagle)

McDonnell Douglas

The little Douglas delta-winged A-4 first flew on 22 June 1954. In service with the Zroa Ha'Avir Ve'Halalal the A-4 was called by the Hebrew name Ahit (Eagle). The A-4 is no stranger to war. The aircraft's combat history can be traced back to the Vietnam War when, as a carrier-borne light attack bomber, it flew countless attack missions into North Vietnam. Known by several nicknames (Scooter, Batman Bomber and Tinker Toy Bomber) the A-4 was flown into the heavily defended skies of North Vietnam by the likes of Lieutenant Junior Grade Everett Alvarez Jr, who was shot down by North Vietnamese anti-aircraft fire to become the first naval PoW of the Vietnam War. This would prove not to be the last A-4 loss in combat.

The embargo on arms sales to Israel by the French produced one very positive outcome for the IASF. Shortly after the Six Day War the Israelis obtained from the United States the A-4 Ahit. The first of the A-4s to arrive in Israel were delivered towards the end of 1967. During the 1960s and 1970s the A-4 Ahit was the primary ground attack aircraft of the IASF, flying innumerable missions during the War of Attrition and the Yom Kippur War. The speed and manoeuvrability of the delta-winged A-4 in the hands of an outstanding pilot also allowed it to be quite capable of protecting itself in air-to-air combat. On 1 May 1967 a former F-8 pilot, Lieutenant Commander Theodore R. Swartz of the United States Navy, flying with VA-76 from the USS *Bon Homme Richard* bagged a North Vietnamese MiG-17 with unguided Zuni rockets. History

The A-4N Ahit was the backbone of the IASF strike fighter force during the 1970s and also participated in combat air operations during the June 1982 Lebanon War. A-4N Ahit 398 in this superb colour photograph carries on its tail the markings of the 'Flying Tiger' squadron. The Hebrew title Ahit Mehupar *(Improved Eagle) is painted on both sides of the jet. The A-4N, besides serving as a bomber for the IASF, also served as one of its pilot training aircraft while assigned to the 'Flying Tiger' squadron. (O. Zidon Collection)*

would repeat itself on 12 May 1970 when the late Colonel Ezra Dotan (Beban) of the IASF downed not one but two Syrian MiG-17s. The colonel, also known as Mister Skyhawk, downed the first MiG with a salvo of anti-tank rockets. The second MiG was taken out with a burst of his A-4's cannon. The cannon rounds ripped off the MiG's left wing sending it into the ground.

Specifications: Douglas A-4 Skyhawk (Ahit – Eagle)

Crew: 1 (2 in OA-4F, TA-4F, TA-4J)
Length: 40 feet 3 inches
Wingspan: 26 feet 6 inches
Height: 15 feet
Empty weight: 10,450 pounds
Load weight: 18,300 pounds
Maximum takeoff weight: 24,500 pounds
Power plant: 1 x Pratt & Whitney J52-P8A turbojet
Maximum Speed: 673mph (585 knots)
Range: 1,700 nautical miles (2,000 miles)
Combat radius: 625 nautical miles
Rate of climb: 8,440 feet/minute
Armament: 2 x 20 mm (0.79in) Colt Mk 12 cannon; 100 rounds per gun
Hardpoints: 4 x under wings & 1 under-fuselage pylon station holding 9,000lbs
Rockets: 4 x LAU-10 rocket pods (each with 4 x 127 mm Mk-32 Zuni Rockets)
Missiles: air-to-air: 4 x AIM-9 Sidewinders; air-to-ground: 2 x AGM-12 Bullpup missiles; 2 x AGM-45 Shrike anti-radiation missiles; 2 x AGM-45 Maverick
Bombs: 6 x Rockeye-11 Mk 20 cluster bomb units (CBU); 6 x Rockeye Mk 7 APAM-59 CBUs; MK-80 series of unguided bombs and B57 & B61 nuclear bombs

F-4E Phantom II (Kurnass – Sledgehammer)
McDonnell Douglas

The Six Day War proved to the air staff of the Zroa Ha'Avir Ve'Halalal that the Air Force was in great need of a truly multi-role fighter. The older aircraft in the inventory, such as the Ouragan, Mystère, Super Mystère and Mirage, had all served with great distinction. However, none could be truly described as a multi-role fighter. A modern aircraft capable of putting bombs on ground targets and yet able to perform in the air-to-air role with a great chance of survival was needed urgently.

At the time this particular photograph was taken Amir Nahumi was a lieutenant colonel in the IASF. He is depicted standing with his ground crew next to an F-16D. Lieutenant Colonel Nahumi would claim fourteen aerial victories during his career with the IASF, and would obtain ace status in both the F-4E and F-16D. (P. Mersky Collection)

During the early to mid-1960s the Israeli government had approached the United States numerous times in an attempt to obtain the combat-tested F-4E Phantom II. It would take until December 1968 for the United States to agree to sell the multi-role Phantom to Israel.

In September 1969, after an extensive training programme, the F-4E Phantom, entered service with No. 102 Squadron at Hatzor. The No. 102 Squadron pilots would be tasked with the most difficult and complex of combat missions. The Kurnass and its aircrew would be involved in attacking highly defended targets, such as air base attack (ABA), battlefield aerial interdiction (BAI), and the most dangerous of all, suppression of enemy air defences (SEAD).

On 9 June 1982 Kurnass pilots proved without a doubt how valuable the acquisition of the Phantom was to the IASF. The Kurnass F-4s were heavily involved in the total destruction of the Syrian Air Defence Force surface-to-air missile sites in the Beqaa Valley. With the destruction of the missile sites the F-4 Kurnasses were able to turn their attention to the important battlefield aerial interdiction mission in support of Israeli ground troops.

During service with the Zroa Ha'Avir Ve'Halalal the F-4E Kurnass and the heroic aircrews who flew into harm's way during the Six Day War, the War of Attrition, and the Yom Kippur War, and countless air battles, proved the versatility of the Kurnass as a bomber and fighter. (In the Ofira air battle two F-4s engaged twenty-eight Egyptian MiG-17s and MiG-21s, shooting down seven and sending the rest away in a hasty retreat.)

On 6 October 1973 the IASF was in a high state of alert anticipating a large-scale attack from Egypt and Syria. Two F-4s from No. 107 Squadron were sitting on alert at Ofira Air Base when, at exactly 1400 hours, Egypt and Syria simultaneously attacked Israel. Israeli

Kurnass No. 653 of No. 119 Squadron, Tel Nof Air Base, carries on its tail the distinctive red chevron of the 'Bat' Squadron. This particular F-4E was upgraded to Kurnass 2000 standards sometime between 1984 and 1989. There is a good chance that the aircraft's original tail number may have been 253. If that is the case Kurnass 653 was credited with a MiG kill while deployed with No. 107 Squadron. A number of F-4Es that underwent conversion to the 2000 standard were known to have acquired MiG kills. (O. Zidon Collection)

ground control units had locked on to a large formation of enemy aircraft approaching from the Red Sea. Defying orders the two Kurnass aircrews (Captain Amir Nahumi and his navigator Yossi Yavin and their wingman Daniel Shaki and navigator David Regev) took off just seconds before the air base at Ofira was attacked by

Specification: F-4E Kurnass (Sledgehammer)

Crew: 2
Length: 63 feet 0 inches
Wingspan: 38 feet 4.5 inches
Height: 16 feet 6 inches
Empty weight: 30,328 pounds
Loaded weight: 41,328 pounds
Maximum takeoff weight: 61,795 pounds
Power plant: 2 x General Electric J79-GE-17A axial compressor turbojet
Maximum speed: Mach 2.23 (1,472mph/2,370km/h)
Cruise speed: 585 mph (506 knots)
Rate of climb: 41,300 feet/minute
Take-off roll: 4,490 feet
Landing roll: 3,680 feet
Armament: Up to 18,650lb of weapons on nine external hardpoints, including general purpose bombs, cluster bombs, TV-and laser-guided bombs, rocket pods, air-to-ground missiles, anti-runway weapons, anti-ship missiles, reconnaissance pods and nuclear weapons.
1 x 20mm M61 Vulcan 6-barrelled Gatling gun with 640 rounds
4 x AIM-9 Sidewinder, Python-3/5 AAMs
4 x AIM-7 Sparrow AAMs
4 x AIM-120 AMRA'AMs
AGM-65 Maverick missiles, AGM-62 Walleyes, AGM-45 Shrikes, AGM-88 HARM missiles, AGM-78 Standard ARMs
GBU15s, Mk-82 GBU12, Mk-84 GBU-10 and CBU-87s

Egyptian aircraft. In the ensuing air battle the F-4 aircrews downed seven enemy MiGs, with four kills being credited to Nahumi and Yavin and three to Shaki and Regev.

The F-4E Phantom II no longer flies with the Zroa Ha'Avir Ve'Halalal having been replaced by the F-15 and F-16 squadrons. However, the accomplishments of the Kurnass aircrews truly added to the legendary status of one of the world's great air forces.

McDonnell Douglas (now Boeing) F-15 Eagle (Baz – Falcon)

The most formidable fighter in the Middle East today is the McDonnell Douglas F-15 Eagle. The F-15 is capable of fighting not only beyond visual range (BVR) but close in air-to-air combat. Designed in the 1960s and 1970s the F-15 was the United States Air Force's answer to the Soviet Union's Mikoyan MiG-25 Foxbat. To date the F-15 has compiled an impressive air-to-air kill record. While in the service of the United States, Israeli and Saudi Arabian Air Forces the Eagle has downed approximately 100 enemy aircraft without a single loss. The first aerial victory credited to the Eagle came on 27 June 1972 when Lieutenant Colonel Moshe Melnik of the IASF's famed 'Double Tail' Squadron, flying F-15 No. 663, downed a MiG-21 of the Syrian Arab Air Force with a Python-3 heat-seeking air-to-air missile.

On 5 June 1984 a Saudi Arabian F-15C intercepted two Iranian F-4E Phantoms that were threatening Saudi oil facilities. One of the Iranian Phantoms was shot down. Some reports indicate that both Phantoms were destroyed during the engagement. During the Gulf War an F-15 of 13 Squadron, Royal Saudi Air Force, flown by Captain Ayed Salah al-Shamrani, engaged, fired on and destroyed two Iraqi Mirage F-1EQ-5s with AIM-9P air-to-air missiles.

The Yom Kippur War was quite short in duration, as wars go, lasting only nineteen days. With the loss of over 100 combat aircraft during the Yom Kippur War it became quite clear to the Israeli General Staff and a number of defence-minded politicians that it was time for the IASF to move quickly to the next generation of fighters if they had any hope of deterring the aggression of the Arab states.

The F-15 Baz in Israeli service is still, without a doubt, the supreme ruler of the skies of the Middle East. The F-15s of the Israeli Air and Space Force and the United States Air Force can claim over 100 aerial combat victories without a single loss. The image of the Baz in this photograph is hazed by the hot jetstream coming from the two powerful Pratt & Whitney F-100 afterburning turbofan engines. The original F-15A/B/C and D models are constantly updated and many have been modified to the point that they are capable of accomplishing missions that were the responsibility of the F-15I Thunder. (O. Zidon Collection)

In June 1974 Israeli Minister of Defence Shimon Peres entered into negotiation with the United States in an attempt to obtain an American-manufactured front-line fighter, which, I'm sure, outraged the French. After many months of public and back-door negotiations the Israelis were granted permission to evaluate two of the United States' front-line fighters, the McDonnell Douglas F-15 Eagle and the Grumman F-14 Tomcat.

Wasting no time the Israelis put together and had on their way to the United States a very impressive evaluation team. That team had among its members a number of outstanding combat pilots with twenty-three MiG kills between the combat pilots and test pilots from the Israeli Aerospace Industry. After putting the Eagle and Tomcat through rigorous testing the team found that the F-15 Eagle emerged as the better fighter. Their decision would prove correct as the F-15 would show itself to be the world's best air superiority fighter in the coming years with the IASF.

The IASF was the first country to engage Soviet-manufactured fighters with the F-15 when, on 26 June 1972, Moshe Melnik of the 'Double Tail' Squadron downed a MiG-21 with a Python-3 air-to-air missile. This incident was just the beginning of the combat history of the F-15 in the Middle East. During the Lebanon War the ISAF would again send the F-15 into action while in the Lebanon War IASF F-15s and F-16s shot down between eighty and ninety Syrian MiG-21s, 23s and MiG-25s (Foxbats). By the 1980s, with the inclusion of the F-16 into the inventory, the ISAF was nearing the completion of the modernization programmes.

The Chel Ha'Avir was, however, still looking to obtain from the United States an extremely manoeuvrable all-weather, deep strike aircraft to engage enemy high-value targets. The one aircraft that fitted the IASF's needs was the United States Air Force's F-15E Strike Eagle.

Specifications: F-15A/B/C/D Baz (Falcon/ Buzzard)

Crew: one
Length: 63 feet 9 inches
Height: 18.5 feet
Wingspan: 42 feet 10 inches
Empty weight: 31,700 pounds
Max takeoff weight: 68,000 pounds
Power plant: 2 x Pratt & Whitney F-100 after-burning turbofan engines
Maximum speed: high altitude Mach 2.5 (1,650 mph/2,660 knots)
Combat radius: 1,061 nautical miles
Service ceiling: 65,000 feet
Rate of climb: 50,000 feet/minute
Guns: one internally mounted 20mm M61A1 Gatling gun with 940 rounds
Hardpoints: four wing, four fuselage, two wing stations, centreline station
Missiles: AIM-9G Sidewinder, AIM-7F Sparrow, AIM-120 AMRAAM, and the Israeli Python missiles

The principal multi-role aircraft in the Zroa Ha'Avir Ve'Halalal is the F-15I Ra'am. F-15I No. 241, like many aircraft in Israel, sits in a hardened shelter, heavily armed with laser-guided bombs and ready at a moment's notice for a deep penetration strike against any would-be attacker. (O. Zidon Collection)

Boeing F-15I Ra'am (Thunder)

During the Gulf War of 1991 Tel Aviv and Haifa were attacked by Iraq-launched SCUD tactical ballistic missiles in an attempt to provoke the Israelis into entering the war. However, after firing thirty-nine SCUDS, which caused very few casualties in Israel, the Israelis remained out of the conflict. The SCUD attacks reinforced Israel's need for an effective long-range strike aircraft. After considering the Lockheed Martin F-16, McDonnell Douglas F/A-18 and F-15E the IASF search for a deep penetration aircraft was solved with the acquisition of the United States Air Force's F-15E Strike Eagle. With a cost of approximately thirty-one million dollars per aircraft the IASF was limited to purchasing only twenty-five F-15Is in 1998. The IASF has dubbed the dual-seat, all-weather highly manoeuvrable fighter-bomber the F-15I Ra'am (Thunder).

The Israeli variant of the Strike Eagle, although outwardly identical (with the exception of the Thunder's desert tan, brown

Specifications: F-15I Ra'am (Thunder)

Crew: 2
Length: 63 feet 9 inches
Height: 18 feet 6 inches
Wingspan: 42 feet 10 inches
Empty weight: 31,700 pounds
Maximum take-off weight: 81,000 pounds
Powerplant: 2 x Pratt & Whitney F100-229 afterburning turbofans, 29,000lb (129 KN) each
Maximum speed: Mach 2.5+ (1,650+mph/2,660+km/h)
Service ceiling: 60,000 feet
Rate of climb: 50,000 feet/minute
Armament: 1 x 20 mm M61 Vulcan Gatling gun, 510 rounds of either M-56 or PGU-28 ammunition
Hardpoints: 2 wing pylons, fuselage pylons, bomb racks on CFTs with a capacity of 24,250lb, external fuel and ordnance

Missiles: 2 x AIM-9M Sidewinders, 2 x AIM-120 AMRA'AMs, 2 x Python 5 AAMs and up to 4 AIM7 Sparrows or additional AIM-120 AMRAMMs, 6 AGM-65 Mavericks, AGM-130s, AGM-84 Harpoons, AGM-84K SLAM-ERs, AGM-154 JSOWs, AGM-158 JASSMs
Bombs: B61 nuclear bomb, Mk82 bomb, Mk84 bomb, CBU-87 CEM, CBU-89 Gator, CBU-97 SFW, CBU-103 CEM,CBU-104 Gator, CBU-105 SFW GBU-10 Paveway II, GBU-12 Paveway II, GBU-15, GBU-24 Paveway III, GBU-27 Paveway III, GBU-28, GBU- 31, GBU-38, GBU-39 small diameter bomb
Changes: A number of modifications have been made to meet IASF requirements: the DASH helmet mounted sight, Israeli Elisra SPS-2110 integrated electronic warfare system, advanced APG-70 radar with terrain mapping. APG-70 regardless of whether, day or night, can locate hard to locate targets

and grey paint scheme) to the F-15E Strike Eagle, is quite different. The F-15I Ra'am was designed with the intention of attacking enemy high value targets deep within the enemy's borders. For its air-to-ground mission the aircraft is equipped with new and unique weapons, avionics, and electronic warfare and communication capabilities. The Thunder is also equipped with the American LANTIRN navigation and targeting pods which enable the F-15I to lock on to targets both day and night. The F-15I was also designed with the ability to defend itself in air-to-air combat. The Ra'am is capable of engaging enemy aircraft with an array of air-to-air missiles, particularly the Rafael Python-5 AAM with its 90-degree

off-bore sight acquisition capability through the use of an Elbit display and sight helmet (DASH) system.

The first two F-15Is arrived on 19 January 1998 and were assigned to the historic No. 69 Squadron at Hatzerim Air Base, located in the Negev desert west of Beersheba. The remaining F-15Is arrived during 1998 and 1999 bringing the total complement of F-15Is in No. 69 Squadron to approximately twenty-five aircraft.

The Ha'patishim (Hammers) of No. 69 Squadron engaged in their first combat missions within just six months of becoming an operational squadron. Two F-15Is armed with GBU-16 Paveway II laser-guided bombs were tasked to attack and destroy

Hezbollah terrorist targets on the Soujud Ridge in southern Lebanon. In February 2000 the Thunder was once again sent into battle, attacking Hezbollah targets in Lebanon. Though not a single word has come forward from the Israeli government to confirm or deny a deep penetration air strike into Syrian territory, it appears that, on 6 September 2007, the F-15I Ra'ams of No. 69 Squadron joined forces with F-16Is for another IASF long-range air strike in Syria.

General Dynamics (now Lockheed Martin) F-16A/B Netz (Sparrowhawk)

F-16C/D Barak (Lightning)

The highly manoeuvrable multi-role F-16 (Sparrowhawk/ Lightning) is a lightweight dogfighter in the true sense of the word. The pilot sits in a reclined seat to reduce the effects of G-forces imposed in the high 9-g turn which the F-16 can sustain. The frameless bubble canopy provides the pilot with outstanding 360-degree visibility. The F-16 is equipped with the M61A1 Vulcan 20mm cannon neatly tucked away in the left wing root. The F-16 is always armed with the AIM-9 Sidewinder or the newer AIM-120 Advanced Medium-Range Air-to-Air Missile (AMRA AM) on each wing tip. The Barak has participated in numerous conflicts, mostly in the Middle East. In fact, the first aerial victory credited to the Falcon was obtained in 1981 by the Zroa Ha'Avir Ve'Halalal on 28 April 1981 when Rafi Raz flying F-16 No. 112 downed a Syrian Mi-8 helicopter. Coincidentally, the first fixed-wing aircraft was also downed on 28 April 1981 when Amir Nahumi flying F-16 No. 219 brought down a Syrian MiG-21.

(On 18 February 1994 NATO warplanes in their first-ever offensive action downed three Serbian G4 Super Galebs. During the engagement Captain Robert Wright of the 526th Fighter Squadron, 86th Fighter Wing was flying F-16 No. 89-2137.

During the Soviet/Afghan war the Pakistan Air Force, flying the F-16, shot down at least ten Soviet and Afghan aircraft that intruded into Pakistani airspace.)

Specifications: (F-16C/D Lightning)

Crew: one
Length: 49 feet 5 inches
Wingspan: 32 feet 8 inches
Height: 16 feet
Empty weight: 18,200 pounds
Loaded weight: 26,500 pounds
Max takeoff weight: 42,000 pounds
Power plant: 1 x Pratt & Whitney F-100-PW-220 after-burning turbofan engine
Maximum speed: at sea level Mach 1.2 (915mph); at altitude Mach 2+ (1,500mph)
Combat radius: 340 nautical miles (295 mi)
Service ceiling: 50,000 feet
Rate of climb: 50,000 feet/minute
Guns: 1 x 20-mm M61A1 Vulcan Gatling gun with 512 rounds
Missiles and bombs: air-to-air: 2 x AIM-7 Sparrows; 6 x AIM-9 Sidewinders; 6 x AIM-120 AMRA'AMs; 6 x Python-4s; air-to-ground: AGM-45 Shrike; AGM-65 Maverick; AGM-88 HARM; bombs: CBU-87, 89 and 97; Paveway series laser-guided bombs: Mks-84, 83 and 82; JDAM munitions: B-61 nuclear bomb

Two F-16As (Nos.126 and 275) from the 'Flying Wing' Squadron stand on quick reaction alert (QRA) equipped with a Pave Penny laser spot tracker. Both of the 'Defenders of the South' Squadron Sparrowhawks in this photograph are armed with unguided general purpose bombs. (O. Zidon Collection)

F-16I No. 407 from the 'Negev' Squadron is seen in this excellent colour photograph decorated in the squadron's new tail art. This F-16I Sufa is configured for both air-to-ground and air-to-air missions. In this photograph 407 is taxiing to take-off at Ramon Air Base. Besides being armed with two laser-guided bombs, the aircraft carries two AIM-120 and two Python air-to-air missiles, a Low Altitude Navigation and Targeting Infra-Red for Night navigation (LANTIRN) pod and three external fuel tanks plus the conformal fuel tank package. (O. Zidon Collection)

No F-16 of any country can claim more aerial victories then the IASF F-16 No. 107. This particular F-16 has been credited with no fewer than six and a half kills and was also flown by Amos Yadlin during Operation OPERA.

F-16I Sufa (Storm)

The F-16Is of the Zroa Ha'Avir Ve'Halalal were obtained to further strengthen the Israeli ability to attack any long-range threats throughout the Middle East, and with their conformal fuel tanks

(CFTs), place Iran well within the reach of IASF aircraft without having to refuel. The F-16I now deployed with the IASF looks radically different from the original F-16. The first two dramatic changes that are apparent are the conformal fuel tanks and larger dorsal spine. The CFTs now fitted to the F-16I extend the range and allow the Israeli fighter to penetrate deeper into enemy airspace.

This extended range allows the F-16I to accompany the F-15I Ra'am on missions to engage high value targets without inflight refuelling. The extended range places Iran well within the reach of both the F-16I Sufa and F-15I Ra'am. The dorsal spine of the F-16I may contain electronic countermeasures equipment (ECM); this, however, is pure speculation as the IASF has never given any indication as to its true purpose. The dorsal spine of the Sufa may contain, amongst other things, the Elisra SPS-3000 self-protection jammer, along with equipment for weapon system delivery capabilities such as smart bombs.

Like the F-15I the F-16I operates with not only American-manufactured weapons but also with variety of locally developed weapons, including advanced Python 4 and 5 air-to-air missiles and Popeye and Spice air-to-ground missiles. Like the F-15I Ra'am the F-16I is jampacked with locally manufactured electronic countermeasures (ECM) equipment, and the new Electro-Optical Guidance (EOPGS) System, allowing direct high precision hits from a much greater distance.

The first two Sufa F-16I (Nos. 407 and 408) arrived in February 2004 and were assigned to the 'HaNegev' Squadron. By 2008 the IASF had three operational squadrons equipped with the new multi-role F-16I attack aircraft.

Chapter Four

Air Combat Weapons – Armament

Air combat over North Vietnam between 1965 and 1972 proved to the United States military complex that the air-to-air missiles in use at the end of the war were less than effective. The kill ratio of the three principal missiles, AIM-7 Sparrow, AIM-9 Sidewinder and AIM-4 Falcon, just did not meet expectation. The original test results of Sparrow and Sidewinder indicated a very high launch-to-kill ratio with Sparrow expected to have a seventy per cent kill rate while Sidewinder was expected to be over sixty per cent. Why then such a poor performance during the Vietnam War? Colonel Marshall L. Michel points out in his outstanding book *Clashes* that the prewar test data may have been flawed. The missiles were never tested in a combat environment nor were they intended for use against a fast-moving, manoeuvring and very nimble MiG-17 or MiG-21, but for use against high-altitude non-manoeuvring bombers.

In the decades since Vietnam the principal aerial interception missiles have been the AIM-7 Sparrow, AIM-9 Sidewinder and the new Advanced Medium-Range Air-to-Air Missile (AIM-120 AMRAAM), all of which have continued to accumulate aerial victories. It would be prudent to mention also the Israeli Python air-to-air missile. The Python is domestically designed and manufactured by Rafael Armament Development. Evolved from the Shafrir air-to-air missile, it proved to be the most successful air-to-air missile during the June 1982 Lebanon War, claiming nineteen of the thirty-three F-15 aerial victories.

The 'Twin Tail' Squadron's F-15D No. 280 is captured in this photograph after completing a combat sortie. Baz 280 is configured for an air-to-air combat air patrol (CAP) mission. The aircraft is equipped with a full complement of four AIM-7 Sparrow radar-guided air-to-air missiles and four Rafael Python 4 AAMs. The roundel painted on the fuselage of No. 280 indicates that this F-15 took part in the 1985 raid on the PLO HQ in Tunis. (O. Zidon Collection)

Raytheon AIM-7M Sparrow

Pilot Brevity Code 'Fox One'

The Raytheon AIM-7M Sparrow missile is a solid fuel, air-to-air guided missile with an eighty-eight-pound blast fragmentation warhead. Sparrow is a medium range semi-active radar-homing missile. Principally employed as a beyond visual range (BVR) weapon, the M model entered service in 1982 with a new inverse monopulse seeker, ECM resistance and a much better low-altitude performance capability. The AIM-7M was the most common Sparrow used during the Gulf War and was credited with most of the American kills. However, the kill probability was less than forty per cent.

Retired Air Force Colonel Marshall L. Michel III, in his book *Clashes*, offers some astounding figures regarding the effectiveness and reliability of the AIM-7 Sparrow during the Vietnam War. Colonel Michel reports that approximately 612 Sparrow missiles (AIM-7s) were fired resulting in fifty-six kills, a success rate of less than ten per cent. Even worse, 404 of the AIM-7s didn't function properly while 152 Sparrows fired missed completely.

The AIM-7, after a long history with both the US Air Force and Navy, is being phased out in favour of the new and more reliable AIM-120 AMRAAM.

Raytheon AIM-9L/M Sidewinder

Pilot Brevity Code 'Fox Two'

The AIM-9 Sidewinder was originally designed for the US Navy as a fleet defence weapon. The first combat use of the AIM-9 was not in the skies over North Vietnam but in the Taiwan Straits. During

> *Specifications: AIM-7M Sparrow*
>
> **Length:** 12 feet
> **Diameter:** 8 inches
> **Wingspan:** 2 feet 8 inches
> **Launch weight:** 500 pounds
> **Engine:** Hercules Mk-85 solid-propellant rocket motor
> **Speed:** Mach 4
> **Range:** 44 miles
> **Guidance:** semi-active radar homing

No F-16 in the free world has more aerial victories to its credit then the 'Flying Wing' Squadron's No. 107. F-16A 107 Netz has accumulated an impressive six and a half air victories. On 7 June 1981 Netz 107 also participated in the IASF raid (Operation OPERA) on the Osirak nuclear reactor near Bagdad. The all-time leading F-16 MiG killer in the IASF is presented in this photograph armed with AIM-9L Sidewinders (Hebrew Deker, or Icepick) air-to-air missiles attached to its wingtips. This historic F-16A obtained all six and a half kills while assigned to the 'First Jet' Squadron during 1982. (O. Zidon Collection)

an air-to-air engagement on 24 September 1958 an F-86 of the Republic of China (Taiwan) Air Force, armed with AIM-9s, downed a Chinese MiG-17. In an unrelated engagement over the Taiwan Straits, one MiG-17 pilot was extremely lucky when an AIM-9 fired at his aircraft failed to detonate and became lodged in the airframe of his MiG. Unfortunately for the United States the MiG pilot was able to land safely which enabled the missile to be recovered by the Russians who reverse-engineered it into the Russian air-to-air AA-2 Atoll missile.

The AIM-9 Sidewinder is a heat-seeking, short-range, all-aspect missile with the ability to attack from all positions, including head-on.

Like the Sparrow the overall performance of the missile was less than impressive during the Vietnam War. United States Air Force and Navy pilots fired approximately 454 AIM-9s at enemy MiGs achieving eighty-one kills. The results are somewhat disturbing when the consequences of the 454 Sidewinders fired are examined. A total of 213 missiles failed, with an additional 160 reported to have missed their targets altogether.

Specifications: AIM-9L/M Sidewinder

Length: 9 feet 4 inches
Wingspan: 2 feet 8 inches
Diameter: 5 inches
Launch weight: 190 pounds
Speed: Mach 2.5
Range: 0.6–11.3 miles
Guidance: infra-red homing
Warhead: 20.8 pound blast-fragmentation

Over 110,000 AIM-9s have been built, which have resulted in approximately 250 to 300 kills worldwide with the best results having been established during the Israel/Lebanon War and the Falklands War. The kill ratio during these conflicts is reported to have been approximately eighty per cent.

Rafael Shafrir 1/2 — Python 4/5

The Shafrir air-to-air missile was built by the Israeli manufacturing company Rafael Armament Development Authority in 1959 and entered service with IASF Mirage squadrons in 1963. In 1978 the Shafrir was given the western name Python.

In 1990 Rafael started development of the Python-5 air-to-air missile (AAM), equipped with an advanced electro-optical

F-16C Barak No. 516 of the 'First Fighter' Squadron based at Hatzor takes off for an air-to-air mission. Tucked under the wings are two Rafael Python air-to-air missiles. The Israeli-designed Python carries a 24.6lb HE blast fragmentation warhead. This Barak is also armed with two Sidewinder air-to-air missiles on its wingtips, and stands ready to engage all air threats. (O. Zidon Collection)

Specifications: Python 4/5

Length: 9 feet 10.1 inches
Diameter: 6.3 inches
Wingspan: 2 feet 9.9 inches
Launch weight: 264.6 pounds
Warhead: 24.6 pound HE blast fragmentation
Engine: one solid-propellant rocket motor
Speed: Mach 2–3.5
Range: 0.5–15 km
Guidance: all-aspect infrared (helmet-mounted sight guidance in later versions)

imaging seeker with lock-on after launch capabilities. The Python is an all-aspect attack capable missile with limited fire-and-forget capabilities as well as helmet-sight guidance. During the Yom Kippur War the IASF launched 176 Python missiles against enemy targets with eighty-nine confirmed kills. Some sources claim that as many as 100 kills were obtained with the Python. The IASF F-15I Ra'am and F-16I Sufa are both capable of deploying the Python AAM in combat.

The Python 5 can also boast a reliability rate greater than ninety-five per cent. Its highly effect warhead, capable of intercepting low-signature/low altitude threats, is also quite effective against most evasive tactics and, as mentioned, it has all-aspect capability, including head-on interception.

Raytheon (Hughes) AIM-120 AMRA AM (Slammer)
Pilot Brevity Code 'Fox Three'

Sufa No. 422 is armed with a lethal combination of Python 4 and AIM-120 air-to-air missiles. This 'Negev' Squadron F-16I is also equipped with conformal fuel tanks (CFT) which extend the aircraft's combat range. The newer AIM-120s have their fifty-pound high explosive blast fragmentation warheads fixed to the aircraft's wing tips. (O. Zidon Collection)

Specifications: AIM-120 AMRA'AM (Slammer)

Length: 12 feet
Wingspan: 20.7 inches
Diameter: 7 inches
Launch weight: 335 pounds
Speed: Mach 4
Range: 30 to 40 miles
Guidance: INS, active radar
Warhead: 50lb HE blast-fragmentation
Engine: Solid-propellant rocket motor in a WPU-6/B Hercules/aero-jet propulsion section

that had turned to engage his flight. Captain North fired one AMRA AM from a forward quarter at about three nautical miles. The kill was not only the first kill for the AIM-120, but the first American F-16 kill (No. 90-0778).

General Dynamics AGM-78D Standard ARM Missile

The General Dynamics AGM-78D ARM was designed to replace the older, less effective AGM-45 Shrike. The AGM-45s were originally designed with a much smaller warhead, limited range and a less than effective guidance system.

During 1973 and 1976 General Dynamics designed and manufactured the newer AGM-78D Standard ARM (anti-radiation missile). The AGM-78D was designed with a new active optical fuse, a newer 220lb blast-fragmentation warhead and a newer more powerful and reliable motor.

In May 1998 the IASF revealed a new F-16D at Hatsor Air Base configured with an AGM-78D, an obvious indication that the IASF

An F-16I deployed with 'One' Squadron sits in a hardened shelter being loaded for an operational mission. Pictured in the foreground is one of the new AIM-120 air-to-air medium range missiles. The AIM-120 has a combat range of between thirty to forty miles. (O. Zidon Collection)

The AIM-120 Slammer is an advanced medium-range air-to-air missile with beyond visual range (BVR) performance capabilities. The AIM-120 is very similar to the Russian R-77 AA-12 Adder, also known in the west as the *AMRAAMski*.

The faster, smaller, lighter AIM-120 has demonstrated better capabilities against low-flying enemy aircraft.

On 29 December 1992 Captain Gary North of the 33rd Fighter Squadron, 366th Fighter Wing claimed the first kill with the AIM-120 air-to-air missile when he downed one of two Iraqi MIG-25s

Specifications: AGM-78D Anti-Radiation Missile

Length: 15 feet 2½ inches
Fin span: 3 feet 3½ inches
Diameter: 1 foot 1½ inches
Weight: 1,350–1,800 pounds (depending on model)
Propulsion: Aerojet Mk 27, mod 4 solid rocket motor
Warhead: 220lb blast-fragmentation type
Fusing: Active optical proximity type
Range: Up to 56 statute miles
Launch speed: Up to Mach 2.0

indeed used the new F-16D and F-16I in the electronic warfare role. The evidence strongly suggests that the AGM-78D anti-radiation missiles were used most effectively in destroying Syrian SAM sites during Operation PEACE FOR GALILEE in Lebanon.

In today's world the list of air-to-air, air-to-ground and air-to-ship missiles seems endless. The author has covered only a small number of the many air-to-air weapon systems in the United States and Israeli inventories.

As with the air-to-air missiles there is no shortage of munitions that go boom in the inventory, from the Mk 80 series of general purpose bombs that have been around for decades, i.e. Mk 82 500lb, Mk 83 1,000lb Mk 84 2,000lb bombs to the CBU-87 Combined Effects Munitions, AGM-154 Joint Stand Off Weapon (JSOW), the laser-guided bombs (LGB) and the newest Global-Positioning-System-guided Joint Direct Attack Munitions (JDAM) kit.

Laser-Guided Bombs (LGB)

(Hebrew Zar'it)

For a long time many were unaware that the laser-guided bombs (LGB) which gained notoriety during the Gulf War were a by-product of the Vietnam era. The LGB is a precision-guided munition (PGM) that uses semi-active laser homing to strike a designated target with greater accuracy. The laser-guided bombs are unpowered weapons that use small wings to guide them towards their targets. The weapon does have one significant problem as laser illumination can be interrupted by a number of sources; fog, smoke or even clouds can limit usefulness in poor weather or very dusty conditions.

The most dramatic example of use of the laser-guided bomb was not in the Gulf War, but in the Vietnam War against the Thanh Hoa

'Hammer' Squadron F-15I No. 241 is one of the Israeli Air Force long-range attack aircraft. No. 241 is loaded with four Zar'it LGBs. The Ra'am is without a doubt the best long-range penetration aircraft in the Israeli Air Force. (O. Zidon Collection)

Bridge, located seventy miles south of Hanoi, a critical crossing point over the Red River. Starting in 1965 US pilots had flown 871 sorties against the Thanh Hoa Bridge, losing eleven aircraft and their valuable aircrews. In all these attempts the United States never managed to put the bridge out of commission. In 1972 the Thanh Hoa Bridge, also known as the 'Dragon's Jaw' bridge, was attacked with laser-guided bombs, and fourteen F-4 Phantoms managed to do what the previous 871 missions had not, 'dropped the span and cut a critical North Vietnamese supply artery'.

Joint Direct Attack Munitions (JDAM)

The Joint Direct Attack Munition (JDAM) made its combat debut during Operation ALLIED FORCE when B-2s flew thirty-hour non-stop round-trip missions from Whiteman Air Force Base, Missouri. During the operation more than 650 JDAMs were delivered on targets with ninety-six per cent reliability and hit eighty-seven per cent of their intended targets.

The Joint Direct Attack Munition is not a weapons system, but a bolt-on upgrade for unguided gravity bombs. The low-cost guidance kit converts unguided gravity bombs, dumb bombs, into accurate, all-weather smart bombs. The JDAM can be released fifteen miles from its target and each GBU-32 (1,000lb bomb) or GBU-32 (2,000lb bomb) can be guided to that target by its integrated guidance system coupled with a global positioning system (GPS) receiver for enhanced accuracy.

The JDAM, which can be deployed from either high or low altitude, is used in close air support, interdiction, offensive counter-air or suppression missions, and the destruction of enemy air defence systems. It is also intended for use against naval anti-surface warfare targets.

Specifications: Joint Direct Attack Munitions (JDAM)

Type: Joint Direct Attack GBU-31 and GBU-38
Length: 9.9–12.75 feet
Wingspan: 16.9 to 25 inches
Range: Up to 15 nautical miles
Used for: Aerial attack fixed targets, precision strike, moving targets

One of the 'First Fighter' Squadron's F-16C Baraks is captured at the moment of lift off. No. 534 is armed with a GPS-guided JDAM kit. (O. Zidon Collection)

Rafael Spice Guided Munitions

The Rafael Spice (Smart Precise Impact, Cost-Effective) weapons system has been in service with the IASF since 2003 with F-16I and F-15I combat squadrons. The electro-optical devices/global positioning system (EO/GPS) guidance kit converts unguided bombs to precision guided bombs. During the pre-flight process of the Spice air-to-surface munitions the missile's computer systems can be fed up to 100 targets to select from during the aircrew's mission. The actual target may be selected inflight by the aircrew. The Spice munitions are satellite guided, giving the weapons a drop-and-forget capability. Rafael Spice munitions are comparable to the American Guide Bomb Unit 15 (GBU-15).

During Operation CAST LEAD (27 December 2008) over seventy Israeli F-15s and F-16s launched air strikes against the Palestinian Hamas Islamic movement in the Gaza Strip. In a matter of minutes the attacking Israeli jets simultaneously attacked over 100 targets. This 'Valley' Squadron F-16D Barak, No. 088, may have participated in CAST LEAD. The squadron is based at Ramat David AB and it is suspected that some of the 'Valley' Squadron multi-role fighters were transferred to other air bases in support of CAST LEAD. In this view of No. 088 the aircraft is seen to be carrying not only Python air-to-air missiles but, neatly tucked under its wings, the Israeli Military Industries Spice guided munition. (O. Zidon Collection)

'Knights of the North' F-16C No. 386 is shown in this February 2004 photograph armed with Rafael Spice precision munitions. The Spice air-to-ground weapon has an operational range of approximately 160 miles and the ability to strike within a matter of feet from its designated target. (O. Zidon Collection)

Specifications: Spice Guided Munitions

Type: Cruise missile
Weight: 550 pounds
Length: 10.9 feet
Diameter: 1 foot 1 inch
Wingspan: 3 feet 9 inches

Operational range: 160 miles
Flight altitude: 28,000 feet
Speed: Mach 0.3–0.7 (Dive: Mach 0.85)
Guidance System: CCD/IIR with GPS/INS
Accuracy: 3 feet 1 inch CEP
Launch platform: aircraft, helicopter, ground launched and sea launched

Israeli Military Industries Delilah Cruise Missile

The Delilah cruise missile was originally designed and developed by the Israeli Military Industries (IMI) as an aerial decoy. Over a period of time Delilah evolved into a highly effective offensive strike weapon. The missile, powered by a turbojet engine capable of Mach 0.85, is air-launched and the stand-off Delilah has an effective combat range of 155.34 miles, and is designed to attack moving and re-locatable targets with a circular error probability (CEP) of three feet three inches.

The Delilah was used effectively by the IASF during operations in Lebanon (July/August 2006) to attack a number of trucks transferring weapons from Syria into Lebanon in support of the Islamic terrorist resistance group Hezbollah. The footage was taken from the Delilah's electro-optic payload.

F-16D No. 601 was photographed in April 2004 armed with the small Delilah cruise missile. The missile is capable of both day and night operation by operator or by GPS guidance system with its day/night electro-optical sensors. (O. Zidon Collection)

F-16I Sufa No. 890 from the 'One' Squadron based at Ramon Air Base emerges from a hardened shelter. The aircraft is armed with two Rafael Python 5 and two AIM-120 air-to-air missiles. Sufa 890 is also armed with two Delilah cruise missiles. The Delilah has a combat range of approximately 160 miles. (O. Zidon Collection)

F-15I No. 238 appears in this September 2004 photograph armed with two IAI Rafael Popeye air-to-ground missiles. The Popeye AGM is guided to its target by the WSO who employs the Popeye's electro-optical guidance system to relay a TV picture from a camera in the nose. (O. Zidon Collection)

AGM-142 Have Nap (Popeye) Cruise Missile

Rafael Advanced Defence System/Lockheed Martin

The AGM-142 Have Nap (Popeye) cruise missile is powered by a single-stage solid-fuel rocket motor. The missile has a built-in inertial guidance system which pilots it towards its target. The standoff capabilities of the Have Nap makes it ideal for attacking large targets, such as power plants, transformers, generators, POL refineries, and radar or communications sites, surface-to-air and anti-aircraft sites. Have Nap can bring two different powerful warheads to the battlefield, 750lb blast/fragmentation or the 800lb penetrator.

There are two variants of Have Nap, one being the Have Lite which has been reduced in size and weight to conform to the F-16. The second variant is the submarine-launched cruise missile (SLCM) Popeye turbo.

Specifications: Delilah Cruise Missile

Type: Cruise missile
Weight: 550 pounds
Length: 10.9 feet
Diameter: 1 foot 1 inch
Wingspan: 3 feet 9 inches
Operational range: 160 miles
Speed: Mach 0.85
Guidance System: CCD/IIR with GPS/INS
Accuracy: 3 feet 3 inches
Launch: Aircraft, helicopter, ground launched, sea launched

Specifications: AGM-142 Have Nap (Popeye) Cruise Missile

Type: Air-to-surface missile
Weight: 3,000 pounds
Length: 15 feet 10 inches
Diameter: 21 inches
Engine: Single-stage solid-fuel rocket
Wingspan: 60 inches
Operational range: 48 miles
Guidance System: Inertial plus IIR or TV
Launch platform: Fixed-wing
Warhead: 750lb blast/fragmentation or 800lb penetrator

Hughes (Raytheon) AGM-65 Maverick

After the poor showing of the Lockheed Martin AGM-12 Bullpup air-to-ground missile during the Vietnam War the United States sought to replace the weapon. The Hughes Aircraft Company, in concert with the Raytheon Company, came up with the design of the AGM-65 Maverick air-to-ground tactical missile. Maverick is perfectly suited for the close air support mission against armour, air defence systems, ground transportation and fuel storage facilities.

In 1982 F-16A No. 250 was assigned to the 'Knights of the North' Squadron when it claimed two Syrian MiGs. The MiG killer is heavily armed in a typical asymmetrical air-to-ground configuration with six Maverick missiles. Though not visible in this photograph you can be sure that there are air-to-air missiles fixed on the aircraft's wingtips for self-defence. The aircraft is positioned in a hardened shelter ready to launch at a moment's notice in defence of Israel. (O. Zidon Collection)

The AGM-65 is a precision attack missile that can be equipped with three different seekers: television, infra-red or laser.

During the 1973 Yom Kippur War F-4E Kurnass fighter-bombers engaged fifty Egyptian targets with Maverick and claimed forty-seven direct hits with the missile. The IASF again used Maverick with great success during the invasion of Lebanon where it engaged twenty different targets with twenty direct hits.

To date the most extensive use of the AGM-65 Maverick has been its deployment during Operation DESERT STORM. During the operation a total of 5,296 Maverick missiles were fired at Iraqi land and naval targets. Maverick was most devastating as an anti-tank weapon with an eighty-five per cent hit rate.

Specifications: AGM-65 Maverick air-to-surface

Type: Air-to-surface guided missile
Weight: 466–670 pounds
Length: 8 feet 2 inches
Diameter: 12 inches
Engine: Thiokol SR-109-TC-1, D, E, F, and G models – SR-114-TC-1 (or Aerojet SR-115-AJ-1) Solid propellant rocket motor
Wingspan: 2 feet 4 inches
Operational range: 15 nautical miles
Guidance system: Electro-optical in A, B, H and K models; infrared imaging in D, F and G models; laser-guided in E models
Launch platform: Fixed-wing
Warhead: 125lb WDU-20B shaped charge – 300lb WDU-24B penetrating blast fragmentation

Chapter Five

Historic Events, Pilots and Aircraft of the Zroa Ha'Avir Ve'Halalal

During times of unlimited national emergency the Israeli Defence Forces (ground, sea and air), despite overwhelming odds, have always been able to defend the State of Israel in support of its national aims.

The following collection of historic IASF aircraft photographs represents just a mere sampling of the aircraft and pilots that have been asked countless times to fly into harm's way in defence of Israel. It seems that it's always the wildest air battles that grab the world's attention, and that many other aspects of the IASF are overlooked. It's not just the fighters of the IASF that have repeatedly demonstrated their superior combat performance, but also the supporting elements of the Air Force. The pre-battle preparations always include the unsurpassed efforts of the electronic countermeasures aircraft, airborne early warning aircraft, transport and utility aircraft, along with in-flight refuelling aircraft.

However, the Zroa Ha'Avir Ve'Halalal (IASF) ability to engage all threats rests entirely with its highly trained and motivated people. With the skills of pilots, listed in this chapter, the air force of Israel should be able to maintain its unsurpassed air dominance in the Middle East for the foreseeable future. Even with the most sophisticated aircraft and weapons at its disposal it will be the troops who will be the final power the next time the Middle East becomes engulfed in war. For the survival of Israel in war has always been a deadly winner-take-all business.

14 July 1966
5 June 1967
6 June 1967
7 July 1969
20 July 1969
11 September 1969
11 November 1969
4 January 1970
6 March 1970
10 July 1970
10 July 1970
13 September 1970
6 October 1973

Mirage III CJ No. 159
No. 101 Squadron, IASF
No. 113 Squadron, IASF
No. 119 Squadron, IASF
No. 110 Squadron, IASF

Captain Yoram Agmon
Captain Ilan Gonen
Captain Uri Shachar
Lieutenant Colonel Oded Maron
Giora Yoeli
Major Giora Aven (Epstein)
Captain Yair Sela
Lieutenant Colonel Oded Maron
Major Yiftah Spector
Major Israel Baharav
Major Avraham Shalmon
Major Eithan Carmi

Mirage III CJ 159: aircraft destroyed: 7 MiG-21s: 2 MiG-17s: 1 MiG-19; 1 Il-14; 1 Su-7; 1 Kelt missile; weapon: 30mm cannon. To describe adequately the combat missions and the thirteen aerial victories credited to this Mirage III CJ would take a book in itself. The first of the thirteen kills was described by Brigadier General Yoram Agmon, for an article that appeared on the Zroa Ha'Avir Ve'Halalal official website.

During 1966 the Syrian government had undertaken a project to alter the course of the waters of the Jordan River. During this project relations with the Syrians were brought to boiling point.

On 14 July 1966 the Israeli Air Force was tasked to put an end to the Jordan River project. The IASF launched the French-built Sud Aviation Vautours (bomber/interceptor) and Dassault Mystère aircraft to carry out air strikes on the primary targets. Protecting the strike force were IASF Mirage III CJs from the 'First Fighter' Squadron. Flying combat air patrol for the strike force, Captain Yoram Agmon was flying in the fourth position in his flight. Agmon continues:

We were scrambled in the direction of the Golan Heights. Suddenly we received instructions from the controller to head westward with the engines at full throttle.

I noticed a shimmering dot at very low altitude, on my left. The dot was advancing in a south-easterly direction, where the Syrian Yarmuk River meets the Sea of Galilee. I informed the flight leader that I had established contact with the enemy, and threw off the detachable fuel tanks.

Without taking his eyes off the target Agmon dived sharply, doing his best to maintain contact with the enemy plane. Flying at high speed, approximately 500 feet from the ground, Captain Agmon positively identified two of the enemy's MiG-21s. In manoeuvring into position Captain Agmon lost sight of the right-hand MiG, and pulled upward in order to slow down and close on the left-hand MiG.

At a range of three hundred and fifty metres I homed in on him for an air attack run. I shot off a short burst, with no results. I immediately executed a second manoeuvre and narrowed the distance between us to two hundred and fifty metres. I aimed the second burst carefully, and immediately saw a powerful explosion in the MiG's right wing. The wing was torn off the plane, which went into a rightward spin. I passed him on his left and saw the pilot bale out. I went westward and joined my quartet near the Sea of Galilee.

Not only was Captain Agmon's aerial victory that Bastille Day of 1966 the first for the Dassault Mirage, it was also the first time that a Russian MiG-21 had been shot down in air-to-air combat. Captain Agmon would end his Air Force career with six aerial victories.

In this black-and-white photograph No. 159 is adorned with thirteen kill markings denoting the eleven Egyptian and two Syrian victories from 1966 to 1973. All thirteen aerial victories were acquired by way of the 30mm cannon. After the thirteenth kill Shahak 159 was given the nick-name 'Bar-Mitsva'. No. 159 is shown in the tail markings of No. 101 Squadron, black, yellow and red. After twenty years of service with the IASF No. 159 was sold to Argentina where the aircraft served with the Fuerza Aerea Argentina. The historic Mirage was eventually sold back to Israel and is now on display at the Israeli Air Force Museum. (A. Dor Collection)

Colonel (Retired) Oded Marom flew Mirage III CJ No. 159 on at least two of his MiG kill missions. Before the Colonel retired from active service he had obtained double 'Ace' status with eleven kills obtained in three wars (Six Day War, War of Attrition and Yom Kippur War). (P. Mersky Collection)

5 June 1967
6 June 1967
6 October 1973

Mirage CJ III No. 103
No. 119 Squadron, IASF
No. 144 Squadron, IASF

Eitan Karmi
Oded Sagi
Uri Yeari
Ran Ron

Mirage CJ III 103: aircraft destroyed: 4 MiG-21s; 1 Su-7; 3 unknown: weapon: 30mm cannon.

Mirage No. 103 is shown in this black-and-white photograph at the end of its service with the IASF. The desert camouflage colour scheme has been replaced with the air superiority grey scheme. This photograph of No. 103 was most likely taken sometime in 1981 at Eitham Air Base. The eight aerial victories credited to it were accomplished between 1967 and 1973. (O. Zidon Collection)

This photograph of No. 158 was taken on 1 June 2004 at Beersheba-Hatzerim, home of the IASF Museum. The tail markings depicted in the photograph are those of the 'First Fighter' Squadron. The black and yellow markings on the tail were placed on the Israeli Shahak jets when other Middle Eastern countries began to deploy the Mirage. (Y. Lapid Collection)

8 June 1967
21 May 1969
2 July 1969
11 December 1969
26 February 1970
2 April 1970
25 April 1970
8 October 1973
12 October 1973
17 October 1973
19 April 1974

Mirage III CJ No. 158
No. 101 Squadron, IASF
No. 119 Squadron, IASF
No. 110 Squadron, IASF
No. 117 Squadron, IASF

Captain Reuven Rozen
Major Eitan Carmi
Captain Menachem Shmul
Lieutenant Colonel Amos Amir
Lieutenant Colonel Oded Marom

Lieutenant Colonel Avi Lanir
Captain Michael Tzuk
Captain Abraham Shalom

Mirage III CJ No. 158: aircraft destroyed: 8 MiG-21s; 4 MiG-17s; 1 Il-28: weapons: 30mm cannon; AIM-9B/E Sidewinder AAMs; Shafrir 2 AAMs. Dassault Mirage III CJ No. 158, like No. 159, has also been credited with a total of thirteen aerial victories over Egyptian and Syrian aircraft from 1967 to 1974. Shahak 158 began service with No. 119 'Bat' Squadron in October 1970 before being transferred to

Mirage III CJ No. 158 appears in this black-and-white photograph parked on the tarmac in front of the national flag of the State of Israel. The number 758 may be seen on the tail of the aircraft. It was, and is to this day, not uncommon to change the tail number when an aircraft in the IASF is transferred from one squadron to another. The photograph depicts only eight of No. 158's thirteen kills which may be an indication that it was probably taken around April 1970. (A. Dor Collection)

No. 101 'First Fighter' Squadron. Eight aerial victories came while No. 158 was assigned to the 'Bat' Squadron. The last kill credited to a Mirage was claimed by No. 158 on 19 April 1974 when Captain Shalmon downed two MiG-21s with 30mm cannon-fire. The eight IASF pilots credited with an aerial victory while flying 158 all went on to become aces in the IASF.

28 April 1970
21 November 1972
13 September 1973
9 October 1973

Mirage III CJ No. 779
No. 119 Squadron, IASF
No. 117 Squadron, IASF

Yitzhak Nir
Zvika Verder
Amos Bar

Mirage III CJ 779: aircraft destroyed: 1 Su-7; 3 MiG-21s; 1 Mi-8: weapons: 30mm cannon; Shafrir-2 AAMs. Shahak No. 779 claimed its first aerial victory on 28 April 1970 when Yitzhak Nir, flying with No. 119 Squadron, engaged an Egyptian SU-7 over the Suez Canal. Nir's aircraft had sustained battle damage prior to engaging the Su-7. Coincidentally, the Su-7 had also been damaged by an air-to-air missile prior to being downed by Shahak 779. Shahak 779 remained with No. 119 Squadron at Tel Nof Air Base until 1970 when it was assigned to No. 117 Squadron. While assigned to No. 117 Squadron this aircraft would add to its aerial victories.

'I decided to use … the air-to-ground rocket pod'

12 May 1970

Douglas A-4N, No. 03
No. 109 Squadron, IASF

Colonel Ezra Dotan

A-4N Ahit (Eagle) 03: aircraft destroyed: 2 MiG-17s: weapon: air-to-ground rockets; 20mm cannon. In southern Lebanon, near the town of Har Dove, Yasser Arafat and the Palestinian Liberation Organization (PLO) terrorists were launching cross-border attacks against the State of Israel. The PLO had effectively taken over the southern part of Lebanon.

On 12 May 1970 the Israeli Army struck back with a major raid against the Palestinian terrorists in 'Fatahland' in southern Lebanon. The Israeli ground force was supported by ten A-4 Ahits (Eagles) of the Israeli Air Force's No. 109 Squadron. The supporting A-4s were all configured to provide close air support to the ground troops engaging the terrorists.

Leading one of the A-4 strike flights was the late Colonel Ezra Dotan, 'Beban', who at the time was no stranger to combat. During 1967, while assigned to No. 117 Squadron, Colonel Dotan had claimed three aerial combat victories while flying the delta-winged Shahak.

During the 12 May 1970 mission Dotan and his flight of A-4s were not looking for MiGs, but tanks. Within moments of identifying a number of enemy vehicles Dotan's wingman identified a flight of enemy MiGs below them. The MiGs were visually identified as Syrian MiG-17s.

Tail markings (red chevron) on Shahak 779 indicate that this particular photograph of the aircraft was taken while assigned to No. 119 Squadron. Two different kill markings have been applied to the nose of the aircraft. One represents the 28 April 1970 kill of an Egyptian Su-7 while the second kill marking indicates that the victim was a Royal Jordanian Air Force aircraft. Looking behind the aircraft you can clearly see painted on the wall (door) of the hardened shelter the Royal Jordanian Air Force insignia. The combat history of Shahak 779 identifies at least five aerial combat victories credited to this aircraft while serving with Nos. 117 and 119 Squadrons. (O. Zidon Collection)

The flight of A-4s quickly descended undetected to a position of advantage behind the Syrian MiGs. The first to engage was Dotan's wingman who engaged the MiGs with cannon-fire, but missed. Dotan then took the lead and engaged the Syrian fighters, not with the A-4's 20mm cannon, but with the air-to-ground rockets.

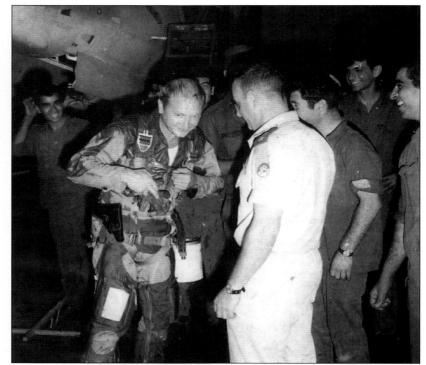

This black-and-white photograph of Colonel Ezra Dotan was taken just a short time after his MiG kill mission of 12 May 1970. One can tell by the smiles on the faces of his ground crew that they were well pleased with the aerial victories of the Colonel and his A-4 Ahit. (A. Dor Collection)

and down it with 20mm cannon-fire. The burst of cannon-fire from his A-4 ripped the left wing off the MiG, which was seen to roll right and hit the ground.

The two Syrian MiG kills on 12 May 1970 were added to three air-to-air victories that Ezra Dotan claimed during 1967, placing him among the elite list of Israeli aces.

USSR vs Israel

30 July 1970

Mirage III CJ, No. 778
F-4E, No. 183

No. 119 Squadron, IASF
No. 69 Squadron, IASF

Major Avraham Shalmon

Aviem Sella
Reuven Reshef
Mirage III CJ (Shahak) No. 778

The first salvo of rockets missed the Syrian MiG passing under the enemy fighter. Dotan repositioned his aircraft and fired a second salvo which destroyed the MiG in one massive explosion. Before the mission was over the late Colonel would engage a second MiG

F-4E Kurnass (Sledgehammer) No. 183: aircraft destroyed: 5 MiG-21s. weapon: AIM-9 Sidewinder AAMs; AIM-7 Sparrow AAMs; 30mm cannon. During 1969 the Egyptians launched the War of Attrition with the State of Israel. The Egyptians started the war in the hope of pressurising Israel into returning land it had captured from Egypt and Syria during the Six Day War in 1967.

By 1970 the Egyptian air defences were unable to stop the IASF from conducting deep penetration air strikes against Egyptian airfields, missile sites, anti-aircraft and artillery positions. President Nasser of Egypt had to request additional arms shipments from the Russians to supplement the weapons and aircraft destroyed by Israel.

The Russians not only re-supplied the Egyptians with surface-to-air missiles but provided an additional eighty MiG-21s, along with pilots, to help defend Egypt's airspace. The missions flown at first by the Russian pilots were in defence of their own air bases, as well as some to defend the capital, Cairo.

IASF pilots were under orders not to approach or otherwise confront the Russian pilots even though, during April 1970, the Russian-piloted MiGs were becoming more aggressive toward IASF aircraft. The uneasy 'ceasefire' came to an abrupt and almost deadly end for an Israeli Skyhawk pilot on 25 June 1970 when an Egyptian, Russian-piloted, MiG-21 intruded into Israeli air space and attacked an A-4 Ahit. Though damaged by a MiG-launched air-to-air missile the Ahit pilot was able to land at a nearby air base.

So much for the 'ceasefire'. With the openly aggressive confrontation initiated by the Russians the IASF set about retaliating and selected twelve of their best fighter pilots who, together, had accumulated fifty-nine aerial victories. The Israeli plan was quite simple: they were going to lure the Russians into attacking what they thought was a flight of A-4 Ahits.

On 30 July 1970 the Egyptian radar site at Sohana in the Gulf of Suez was attacked by a flight of F-4E Kurnass strike aircraft. The Israelis had positioned a flight of four high-flying Mirage III CJs above the attacking F-4s and a second flight of F-4Es configured with air-to-air missiles below the attacking F-4s. Positioned further to the rear were four additional Mirage delta-winged fighters waiting for the Russians to show themselves. When the Soviets failed to respond, the lead section of Israeli Mirage fighters simulating an A-4 flight profile continued farther into Egypt in an attempt to force the Soviets into acting. When the Soviets finally scrambled eight MiG-21s from the 135th IAP, led by a Captain Kamencev, the trap had been sprung and the air battle was about to begin. What Captain Kamencev and the rest of his flight were totally unaware of when they scrambled was that they were being led by IASF Mirage fighters, and not A-4 Ahits, into a trap. An additional four MiG-21s were also scrambled from Kom Awshim and four more from Kutamiyah to join in the air battle.

The second section of IASF Mirage fighters and the F-4Es from 69 'Hammer' Squadron were about to join in the fray.

During the air battle two F-4Es from 69 Squadron, flown by Aviem Sela/Reuven Reshef and Avihu Ben-Nun/Shaul, each claimed a MiG-21. Three Mirage III aircrews from 119 Squadron (Asher Snir, Abraham Shalom and Yiftah Spector) shared a claim for the fifth MiG.

Aviem Sela provided details of his kill in an interview for the Israeli Press:

I started looking for a MiG to kill. Finally, found one, its pilot making a right turn, trying to close in on my number one who broke to the right. The MiG left my number one and started chasing me! We stuck together for a while, dropping to about 15,000 feet; at that point he was only about 150 metres from me. I could see the pilot's helmet clearly.

By this time I'd realized the Russian pilot was inexperienced; he didn't know how to handle his aircraft in a combat situation. At 15,000 feet he proved this fact by trying to escape in a steep dive to 7,000 feet. All we had to do was follow him and lock our radar onto him – and fire a missile. There was a tremendous explosion, but the MiG came out of the cloud of smoke apparently unharmed. That made me mad and I fired a second missile which turned out to be unnecessary. The Russian aircraft had, in fact, been severely damaged by the first missile; suddenly it burst into flames and fell apart. By the time the second missile reached it, it wasn't there anymore.

After the loss of five MiGs the Russian beat a hasty retreat back home with the Israeli fighters giving chase. The Israeli air controller recalled the IASF fighters before any additional kills were made. However,

The late Brigadier General (Retired) Asher Snir was one of the Zroa Ha'Avir Ve'Halalal's most highly-respected fighter pilots. During his military career the General was credited with thirteen and a half aerial combat victories while flying the Mirage and the F-4E Kurnass. While no evidence exists to suggest that any of his aerial victories came while flying Mirage No. 778, however, his shared kill came about during the Israeli/Russian air battle of 30 July 1970. General Snir flew his last combat mission in October 1985 during the long-range strike against the PLO headquarters in Tunis. He passed away on 5 October 1986. (P. Mersky Collection)

The 'Bat' Squadron's ground crew prepares Mirage III CJ No. 778 for another combat mission. No. 778 was the jet flown by Abraham Shalom on 30 July 1970 when he downed two of the Russian-flown EAF MiG-21s with AIM-9D Sidewinder air-to-air missiles. Before being shot down by Syrian AAA fire on 10 October 1973 this historic Mirage would claim additional aerial victories: 9 September 1972, Yoram Geva, 1 Syrian Arab AF Su-7; 11 September 1972, Abraham Shalom, 1 Syrian MiG-21; 13 September 1973, Israel Baharav, 2 Syrian MiG-21s. (O. Zidon Collection)

another Russian-flown Egyptian MiG, which had sustained battle damage, crashed while landing. The Israelis did everything correctly; the ambush of the Russians was executed brilliantly.

After action reports indicate that, of the five Russian pilots shot down, Captains Vladimir Zuravey, Nikolay Yurchenko and Evgeny Yakovlev were all killed in action. One pilot ejected and was rescued and the fifth pilot ejected but died under his parachute.

F-4E Kurnass (Sledgehammer)

The Mirage is undoubtedly the most famous and legendary aircraft to serve in the Zroa Ha'Avir Ve'Halalal. Joining the IASF inventory on 7 April 1962 to counter the Soviet MiG-21s the Mirage

Pictured here is the jet flown by Aviem Sella and Reuven Reshef on 30 July 1970 when they engaged, fired on and destroyed an Egyptian MiG-21 flown by a Russian pilot. The aircraft in the photograph is marked with two kills. The second kill was obtained on 9 September 1972 by Avihu Ben-Nun and Zvi Edan when they downed a Syrian Su-7 with an AIM-9D Sidewinder air-to-air missile. Coincidentally, Avihu Ben-Nun downed one of the Russian-piloted MiG-21s while flying No. 105.

On 24 July 1982 No. 183 was hit by a Syrian SA-8 missile while operating over the Beqaa Valley in eastern Lebanon. WSO Aharon Katz was killed and pilot Gil Fogel ejected and was captured and held by the Syrians for over two years. (O. Zidon Collection)

III CJ proved itself to be a world-class interceptor in the hands of the right pilot. During its service with the IASF the Mirage III CJ has claimed 282.5 confirmed aerial victories over Arab aircraft. However, the primary mission of the IASF is to put bombs on the targets of their enemies and destroy their will to fight. As a bomber the Mirage's performance was limited, it suffered from limited range, limited weapons load, and its all-weather performance was less than satisfactory.

Looking to the United States the State of Israel sought to obtain the versatile F-4 Phantom II. Proven in combat during the Vietnam War as a multi-role fighter the Phantom was able to present itself as an outstanding ground attack aircraft with the capability of placing seven tons of bombs on its targets. This far surpassed the Mirage which was only able to place one ton of ordnance on the target. Not only was the Phantom able to attack ground targets but it was more than able to defend itself in aerial combat. From September 1969 to June 1982 the F-4 Phantom would claim 116.5 MiG kills in the hands of Israeli pilots. The kill-to-loss ratio from November 1969 to September 1973 was twenty-five to one; in the Yom Kippur War, eighty-five to one; and from December 1973 to June 1982 six point five to zero.

Called the Kurnass by the Zroa Ha'Avir Ve'Halalal the F-4E Phantom entered combat with the Israelis within a matter of days. The first F-4s announced their presence in the Middle East when, on 11 November 1969, Captain Ehud Hankin and Major Eyal Achikar of 201 Squadron claimed the first aerial victory in the Kurnass over an Egyptian Air Force MiG-21. Hankin and Achikar were flying F-4E Kurnass No. 608.

During the Lebanon War of 1982 the IASF's F-4E 'Bat' Squadron was tasked to lead the way in destroying the Syrian surface-to-air missile batteries in the Lebanon Valley. The air strikes were designed to take out the missile sites and their controlling radars. The missions were so successful that the IASF's F-15 Baz and F-16 Netz aircraft were able to deal at will with the Syrian Arab Air Force MiGs.

Most F-4E Kurnass aircraft in service with the IASF have, like the Mirage and Nesher, passed into Israeli aviation history. There are, however, some Kurnass F-4Es that have obtained legendary status and are presented herein.

11 November 1969

F-4E, No. 608
Nos. 201/69 Squadrons, IASF

Captain Ehud Hankin
Major Achikar Eyal

F-4E Kurnass (Sledgehammer) No. 608: aircraft destroyed: MiG-21: weapon: AIM-9D Sidewinder AAM. IASF Mirage IIIs took off from Hatzor Air base to patrol the area of Jabel Ataka when they engaged two Egyptian MiG-21s. In the ensuing air battle the two MiGs were shot down. Also operating with the six Mirage interceptors were two IASF F-4Es from Nos. 201/69 Squadrons. Captain Ehud Hankin and his navigator Major Achikar Eyal were paired in Kurnass 08 (No. 608) while their flight leader Yoram Agmom and Menachem Eini were teamed in Kurnass 10. The pair of F-4Es picked up four bandits whom they visually identified as EAF MiG-21s. Major Achikar Eyal described the kill in an article on the Zroa Ha'Avir Ve'Halalal website:

The controller informed us that there were Egyptian MiGs north of us, and instructed the Israeli Mirage fighters to turn towards the MiGs and engage. Meanwhile, we and the other Phantom in our flight opened the afterburners and crossed the Red Sea at high speed, entering Egypt at low altitude.

We pulled upward and identified a quartet of MiG-21s. Our partner picked out one of the MiGs and we chose another one. Hankin shot off an accurate missile. The MiG was hit, lit up in flames and started spinning downward wildly. The pilot baled out … We had plenty of fuel and could have gone after more MiGs, but the flight controller ordered us to return home immediately.

With the MiG-21 kill of Hankin and Eyal, the Kurnass had established itself in the War of Attrition as being quite capable not only of being a bomber but also as a dogfighter, enhancing the reputation gained in Vietnam.

In this black-and-white photograph Kurnass No. 608 is depicted with landing gear down just prior to landing. Painted on the fuselage just under the forward part of the canopy is the MiG kill marking denoting the aerial victory of Hankin and Eyal on 11 November 1969. This historic F-4E was one of the first four Phantoms delivered to Israel under the 'Peace Echo' programme. This Kurnass began service with the 'One' Squadron and now sits in the IASF Museum junkyard. F-4E Kurnass 609 was lost on 4 June 1978 when it collided with an IASF A-4 Skyhawk. The A-4 pilot was killed while the two-man crew of No. 609 was able to eject. (O. Zidon Collection)

13 September 1973

F-4E, No. 184
No. 107 Squadron, IASF

Major Yiftah Spector
Micha Oren

F-4E Kurnass (Sledgehammer) 184: aircraft destroyed: 3 MiG-21s: weapon: AIM-9D Sidewinder AAMs. By the time Spector and Oren destroyed two Syrian MiG-21s on 13 September 1973 Spector was already an ace with eight aerial victories from his time flying the Mirage III.

Kurnass No. 184 was changed to No. 584 when the aircraft was modified to Kurnass 2000 status. The jet, however, has retained the MiG kill markings obtained while it carried No. 184. In this old, undated photograph ground personnel are busy preparing the MiG killer for an air-to-ground training sortie. (O. Zidon Collection)

On 13 September 1973 the Commanding Officer (CO) of No. 107 Squadron, Major Yiftah Spector, and his navigator, Micha Oren, were flying a combat air patrol mission for an IASF reconnaissance flight when they engaged and destroyed two MiG-21s of the Syrian Arab Air Force. Both MiG-21s were shot down with heat-seeking Sidewinder air-to-air missiles. With two confirmed MiG-21 kills on 13 September 1973, Spector became a double ace with ten kills. He would eventually be credited with fifteen kills making him the second highest scoring ace in the IASF.

Yom Kippur War 1973

6 October 1973
13 October 1973
16 October 1973
23 October 1973

F-4E, No. 109
No. 201 Squadron, IASF
No. 69 Squadron, IASF

Lieutenant Colonel Ben-Ami Peri
Itzhak Amitay

Captain Yoram Among
Daniel Wittmann

Dani Halotz
Yehoar Gal

F-4E Kurnass (Sledgehammer) No. 109: aircraft destroyed: 3 Mi-8s; 4 MiG-21s: weapons: 20mm cannon; AIM-9 Sidewinder AAMs; AIM-7 Sparrow AAMs. The first three kills credited to No. 109 came on 6 October 1973 when Lieutenant Colonel Ben-Ami Peri and his navigator, Itzhak Amitay, downed three Egyptian Mi-8 helicopters. Peri and Amitay were part of a four-plane CAP mission when their ground control interception operator (GCI) vectored them on a direct course to intercept the Egyptian Mi-8s. 'There they are.' And there they were – six Mi-8s in a perfect formation. Peri and Amitay downed three of the helicopters with 20mm cannon-fire while other members of the flight downed the remaining enemy aircraft.

This black-and-white photograph of the king of all F-4E Phantom MiG killers was shot while No. 109 was serving with the IASF. This historic MiG killer claimed seven aerial victories. The boom protruding from the fuselage of No. 109 is for in-flight refuelling. The jet can be refuelled by either a Boeing 707 Re'em or the KC-130 Karnaf. The tail markings on 109 indicated that, when this photograph was taken, it was assigned to the 'Bat' Squadron. (A. Dor Collection)

For years the delta-winged Mirage fighters of the IASF were the unchallenged MiG Killers of the Middle East. During the Yom Kippur War the F-4E Kurnass was given the chance to challenge. However, that challenge fell short as the Kurnass fighter-bombers would only claim approximately 116 aerial victories during service with the IASF. The all-time leading Kurnass MiG killer is No. 109 with seven confirmed kills. In this black-and-white photograph Israeli airmen stand proudly next to 109 with the seven kill markings visible on the nose of the aircraft.

Unfortunately, this historic aircraft was lost as the result of a mid-air collision with an A-4 of the IASF. (O. Zidon Collection)

Seventeen days after Peri and Amitay killed the three Mi-8s in No. 109 the aircrew of Dani Halotz and Yehoar Gal claimed two Syrian MiG-21s. The pair were flying in the number three position in Tiger flight. Tiger 03 was in a position to see Tiger 04, Chaim Rotem, making a gun pass on a MiG. Tiger 04 was not hitting the MiG so 'Halotz asked Rotem, "Will you please step aside?"' As soon as Tiger 04 broke off Halotz launched an AIM-9 which tracked to the MiG and in an instant destroyed the enemy aircraft. Shortly after their first kill Halotz and Gal engaged a second MiG which they downed with a Sparrow radar-guided missile at a range of 2,000 metres.

6 October 1973
10 October 1973
14 October 1973

F-4E, No. 222
No. 107 Squadron, IASF

Dani Shaki
David Regev

Naftaly Maimon
Oded Poleg

Major Yiftah Spector
Roy Manof

F-4E Kurnass (Sledgehammer) 222: aircraft destroyed: 2 MiG-17s; 3 MiG-21s: weapons: AIM-9D Sidewinder AAMs. On the first day of the Yom Kippur War, 6 October 1973, a combined assault by

Egypt and Syria against Israeli forces in the Sinai desert and Golan Heights was supported by the Egyptian and Syrian Arab Air Forces. One of the initial air battles was the Ofira air battle, involving two

A unique black and white photograph of IASF personal posed next to Kurnass No. 122. The photograph depicting the faces of Chel Ha'Avir personal has been cleared by the government censor. No. 122 was changed to Kurnass 222 but still carried markings for the aircraft's five aerial victories from the Yom Kippur War. Appearing in the photograph are Yiftach Spector, fourth from the left, and Roy Manof, second from the left, who claimed a kill in 122. Also present is Dani Shaki, sixth from the left. This ace of the IASF began its service with the 'Orange Tail' Squadron as 122 when it claimed its five kills. On 20 January 1981 this aircraft collided with an F-16A Netz from the 'Knights of the North' Squadron. In a weird coincidence both planes were numbered 222 at the time of the accident. (Yossi Ye'ari via T. Ben-Ami)

Standing alone Kurnass No. 222 appears in this black-and-white photograph in a clean (no ordnance) condition. Though No. 222 may appear somewhat serene in this photograph one can't help but notice the five roundels attesting to the lethal nature of this historic MiG killer. (O. Zidon Collection)

Israeli F-4E Kurnass fighters against twenty-eight Egyptian MiGs. In six minutes two F-4Es killed seven enemy aircraft. Four of the enemy MiG-17s were claimed by Amir Nahumi and Yosef Yavin, flying Kurnass No. 181, and three by Dani Shaki and David Regev in No. 122. (No. 122 was changed at some point to No. 222)

Kurnass No. 122 went on to claim two additional Syrian MiG-21s during the Yom Kippur War. On 10 October 1973 Naftaly Maimon and Oded Poleg of No. 107 Squadron engaged and destroyed a MiG-21 with an air-to-air missile while Yiftah Spector and Roy Manof claimed a fifth MiG with an AIM-9D AAM on 14 October.

6 October 1973

F-4E, No. 151
No. 107 Squadron, IASF

Lieutenant Shlomo Egozy
Roy Manof

F-4E Kurnass (Sledgehammer) No. 151: aircraft destroyed: 5 Mi-8s: weapon; 20mm cannon. 'The second major Egyptian Air Force action on the first day came at dusk with a commando assault involving dozens of Mi-8 helicopters. Seven of the Mi-8s were downed by Phantoms from the No. 107 Squadron, Orange Tails, including one deliberately driven into the ground by the jet-wash from a Phantom's afterburners.' The mission of the Egyptian helicopters was to penetrate the Sinai and deploy Egyptian commandos. The mission of the approximately 300 commandos was to attack rear area targets in Israel.

The low-flying Mi-8s were discovered by Israeli ground control radar. F-4Es of the 'Orange Tail' Squadron located the attacking Egyptian helicopters at the last minute and prevented them from unloading their troops in the rear areas.

The attacking IASF F-4Es totally devastated the Mi-8s, shooting down between twelve and fourteen of the enemy aircraft. Senior deputy CO Shlomo Egozy and his navigator Roy Manof claimed five kills flying Kurnass 151. Four kills were made with cannon-fire and the fifth 'using the blast from their jets' exhausts, smashing the helicopter to the ground as they pulled up in full afterburner.'

6 October 1973
13 October 1973
14 October 1973

F-4E, No. 230/630
No. 107 Squadron, IASF

Dubi Yoffe
Moshe Pereg

Dani Halotz
Shimon Noi

Lieutenant Shlomo Egozy
Yosef Yavin

Kurnass No. 151 appears in this black-and-white photograph on static display during an open house at the home base of the 'Orange Tail' Squadron. On 6 October 1973 the crew of Egozy and Manof of the No. 107 Squadron flew this aircraft and downed five Mi-8s in a single air battle. Kurnass 151 was shot down on 12 October 1973 while on an air base attack (ABA) mission to Damascus, Elmaza air base. The pilot Ran Goren and navigator Micah Oren were able to eject over Israeli territory where they were quickly located. (Y. Ye'ari Collection via T. Ben-Aim)

F-4E Kurnass (Sledgehammer) No. 230: aircraft destroyed: 1 Mi-8; 1 MiG-21; 1 MiG-17: weapons: 20mm cannon; AIM-9D Sidewinder AAMs. Another of the IASF F-4Es credited with a Mi-8 kill on 6 October 1973 was Kurnass No. 230 (later changed to No. 630) flown by Dubi Yoffe and his navigator Moshe Pereg. Fortunately for the Zroa Ha'Avir Ve'Halalal they had spent time training their pilots to deal with attacking helicopters as these proved to be difficult targets. The low-flying, slow moving Mi-8s had to be brought down by cannon-fire.

On 13 October 1973 Dani Halotz and his back-seater, Shimon Noi, were vectored to intercept Egyptian Su-7s in the Bitter Lake sector. The Su-7s were being escorted by EAF MiG-21s. Halotz went after one of the MiG-21s and locked the MiG up with an AIM-9D and, after establishing a good tone indicating that the missile was locked on, fired. Scratch one MiG-21. While Halotz and Noi were engaged, their wingman, Gil Regev and Ilan Lazar, destroyed an EAF Su-7.

Shlomo Egozy, 107 Squadron senior deputy CO, claimed his eighth Kurnass kill on 14 October 1973 flying Kurnass 230. Lieutenant Egozy and his navigator Yosef Yavin shot down the Syrian MiG-17 in what has been described as an old fashioned dogfight, ending with the destruction of the MiG with 20mm cannon-fire.

During the Yom Kippur War F-4E Kurnass No. 230 was assigned to No. 107 Squadron and credited with three aerial victories. After the war No. 230 was modified and upgraded to Kurnass 2000 standards. During the upgrade the number 230 was changed to 630. In the first of two outstanding colour photographs, Kurnass 630 sits on the tarmac with other IASF aircraft still proudly sporting the three roundels signifying Kurnass 630's aerial victories from the Yom Kippur War.

6 October 1973

F-4E, No. 171
No. 201 Squadron, IASF

Lieutenant Colonel Eitan Peled
Abraham Ashael

F-4E Kurnass (Sledgehammer) No. 171: aircraft destroyed: 2 Mi-8s: weapon: 20mm cannon. One can only imagine what the consequences could have been if the 300 Egyptian commandos had

been able to pull off their rear area assault during 6 October 1973. If it hadn't been for the timely arrival of the Phantoms these troops would have faced lightly defended targets as most Israeli ground troops had been committed to the front and were heavily engaged with Egyptian and Syrian forces.

Eitan Peled and his navigator, Abraham Ashael, were leading a four-plane flight of Phantoms from Tel Nof when they engaged, fired on and destroyed two of the Egyptian Mi-8s before they had a chance to land and unload their commandos.

In the second photograph Kurnass No. 630 is captured heading out in a full afterburner take off. When this historic jet claimed its aerial victories it was assigned to No. 107 Squadron. In these two photographs the tail markings are those of the 'One' Squadron. This particular photograph was taken in 2004 at the Tel-Nof Air Base. (O. Zidon Collection)

Peled and the other Kurnass aircrews found that ground strafing tactics with the 20mm cannon were more successful in taking out the enemy helicopters. It was near impossible to lock-on to the low-flying, slow moving Mi-8s with radar and at such low altitude the AIM-9 wasn't very effective.

13 October 1973
16 October 1973
23 October 1973

F-4E, No. 209
No. 69 Squadron, IASF
No. 201 Squadron, IASF

Yoram Agmon
Daniel Wittmann
Dani Halotz
Yehoar Gal

Kurnass No. 171 of the 'Bat' Squadron is seen taxiing after landing at Tel Nof Air Base, home of No. 119 Squadron. In this photograph No. 171 appears in the standard IASF three-shade camouflage. For a short time in the mid-1980s No. 119 Squadron had applied the blue tail flash to their F-4Es. Kurnass 171 was modified to Kurnass 2000 standards and re-numbered as 671. This is the same two-seat multi-role strike fighter flown by Peled and Ashael on 6 October 1973 when they downed the two EAF Mi-8 helicopters. (O. Zidon Collection)

F-4E Kurnass (Sledgehammer) No. 209: aircraft destroyed: 1 MiG-17; 3 MiG-21s: weapons: 3 AIM-9D Sidewinder AAMs; 1 AIM-7 Sparrow AAM. At midday on 13 October 1973 No. 69 Squadron F-4s were launched to intercept Syrian MiGs that were attacking Israeli ground troops who were engaged heavily with Syrian units on the Golan Heights. Upon arriving in the skies over the Golan Heights Yoram Agmon and his navigator Daniel Wittmann engaged a MiG-17. During the engagement Agmon and Wittmann experienced a malfunction and were unable to launch their air-to-air missile. Without hesitation Agmon ordered his navigator to launch a second missile. This heat-seeker missile came off the rail and tracked directly to the enemy MiG, hitting with a violent explosion that destroyed the Syrian aircraft.

On 16 October 1973 Yoram Agmon and Daniel Wittmann were on their way home after successfully completing an air strike on an important tank repair workshop. The F-4 Kurnass squadrons were intercepted by Syrian MiGs. In the ensuing air battle Agmon and Wittmann claimed their second MiG within a matter of days when they downed a MiG-21 with a heat-seeking Sidewinder.

Two additional MiG kills were credited to Kurnass 209 on 23 October 1973 when Dani Halotz and Yehoar Gal downed two MiG-21s during a mission to destroy a Syrian strategic oil storage area.

14 October 1973

F-4E, No. 101
No. 107 Squadron, IASF

Naftaly Maimon
Yitzhak Raz

F-4E Kurnass (Sledgehammer) No. 101: aircraft destroyed: 2 MiG-21s: weapons: AIM-9D Sidewinder AAM; 20mm cannon. On 14 October 1973 Maimon and Raz were flying in (call sign) 'Bed' section on a strike mission against Tanta Air Base. The attacking F-4s were each armed with five Mk-117 750lb bombs, four Sparrow and one Sidewinder air-to-air missiles.

On approach to Tanta Air Base, located on the western side of the Nile Delta, the F-4Es were engaged by MiG-21s. The aggressiveness of the EAF MiG pilots forced many of the F-4s in 'Buffet' and 'Bed' section to jettison their bombs. Maimon reported, 'I pushed the

The MiG killer Kurnass No. 209 appears in this photograph marked with four Syrian kill markings denoting the aerial victories of two different aircrews during the Yom Kippur War. The date of this particular photograph of 209 is unknown but it must have been taken after the double MiG kill mission of Halotz and Gal over Khan Ayish. No. 209 is marked with the four Syrian roundels indicating the jet's combat victories. The roundels are meant to indicate the combat record of the aircraft and not a particular pilot. (O. Zidon Collection)

Kurnass No. 101 appears in this colour photograph in formation with F-4Es from No. 107 Squadron during a fly-past over Jerusalem during Israel's 25th Independence Day celebration in 1973.

The second in-flight photograph captures the double MiG killer flying in formation with two other F-4Es from the 'Hammer' Squadron from Ramat David Air Base. The distinctive black and yellow check pattern and squadron badge are present on the tail of the aircraft.

Kurnass No. 101 was the very first F-4E Phantom delivered to the IASF. (Y. Yarria / A. Dor Collections)

panic button to clean off the aircraft of all external stores. I heard a boom and for a moment I thought we'd been hit.'

In the ensuing air battle Bed 3, Naftaly Maimon and Yitzhak Raz, flying what they thought was a damaged aircraft, engaged a number of EAF MiGs and claimed and were credited with shooting down two of the enemy fighters. The first kill was accomplished with an AIM-9D Sidewinder while the second MiG was taken with the internal 20mm cannon at 700 to 800 metres. Maimon is quoted in

Shlomo Alonis's book *Israeli F-4 Phantoms*, 'The MiG didn't explode in a fireball, but simply stopped flying in a huge-G pitch up.'

It wasn't until they landed that Bed 3 learnt that they weren't hit, but were still carrying bombs and the external fuel tanks below the right wing which failed to jettison when they hit the panic button.

3 January 1982

RF-4E(S), No. 498
No. 119 Squadron, IASF

Shablool (Snail) No. 498 has painted on its nose an Iraqi Air Force symbol denoting its aerial victory of 3 January 1982 over a MiG-21. In this striking photograph No. 498 is depicted in the tail markings of the 'One' Squadron which flew the Kurnass for almost thirty-five years. The RF-4E(S) recce birds gathered at Tel-Nof Air Base for the formal farewell parade on 12 May 2004.

In this ground shot photograph No. 498 is starting to show a little age as the three-tone paint scheme is beginning to fade. The tail flash identifies 498 as being assigned to the 'Bat' Squadron. In this photograph the aircraft's long-range oblique photograph camera is shrouded with a black cover.
RF-4E(S) No. 498 was the only RF-4E to be credited with an aerial victory during its service with the IASF. (O. Zidon / T. Ben-Aim Collections)

Gideon Sheffer
Yuval Naveh

RF-4E(S) Shablool (Snail) No. 498:   aircraft destroyed: MiG-21: weapon: manoeuvre. On January 1982 two IASF RF-4E(S)s were tasked with a highly classified reconnaissance mission over Iraq when an Iraqi Air Force MiG-21 attempted to intercept them. After completing their photo run the pair of RF-4Es enticed the MiG pilot into pursuing them. Gideon Sheffer and navigator Yuval Naveh guessed correctly that the MiG pilot was in full afterburner since being scrambled and all they had do was keep him in the air a little longer and he would run out of fuel.

Sheffer and Naveh tactically manoeuvred their aircraft, never giving the MiG pilot an opportunity to launch an air-to-air missile in their direction. The pair caused the destruction of the MiG-21 without firing a single shot.

Chapter Six

Enter the F-15 Eagle/Baz (Falcon)

Like the Mirage III, Nesher, Skyhawk and many other aircraft deployed by the Zroa Ha'Avir Ve'Halalal, the F-4E Phantom II will no longer be seen patrolling the skies of the Middle East. After thirty-five years, and countless confrontations with Israel's enemies, the legendary F-4E Kurnass is being phased out of combat service.

The Israeli government approached the United States in an attempt to obtain a replacement for the aging F-4E. The United States Department of Defense (DoD), and the Zroa Ha'Avir Ve'Halalal, after months of negotiation, did agree on two possible replacements for the F-4E. The two fourth-generation fighters offered by the United States were the Air Force's F-15, and the Navy's F-14. After comparing the F-15 Eagle and the F-14 Tomcat the IASF selected the F-15 Eagle as its air superiority weapons platform, and the United States Air Force's Lockheed Martin F-16 Falcon for its air-to-ground needs.

The first IASF F-15 Baz unit was the 'Double Tail' Squadron which was activated at Tel-Nof Air Base on 28 November 1976.The F-15 Baz would claim its first aerial victory on 27 June 1979, when Major Moshe Melnik, flying with the 'Double Tail' Squadron, killed a Syrian Arab Air Force MiG-21 with a Python-3 air-to-air missile. During the mission Major Melnik was flying F-15A No. 663, nicknamed 'Hamadlik' (Fire Igniter). The major not only claimed the first kill in the F-15, but also introduced the Israeli system of naming individual F-15s.

The F-15 Baz air-to-air exchange ratio of forty-five and a half to zero (45.5 to 0) with the IASF is impressive, but killing MiGs is only one of the F-15's capabilities. On 1 October 1985 eight IASF F-15s crossed the Mediterranean on a bombing mission to strike the PLO headquarters in Tunis. The Israeli pilots, attacking in two waves, scored direct hits on the PLO complex destroying almost the entire complex.

27 June 1979

F-15A, No. 663
Hamadlik / Fire Igniter
Double Tail Squadron

Major (later Brigadier General) Moshe Melnik

F-15A-17-MC 76-1508 No. 663: aircraft destroyed: MiG-21: weapon: Python-3 AAM. Retired Brigadier General Moshe Melnik supplied the following account of the first ever kill for the F-15 Baz to the Israeli Air Force official website.

On 27 June 1979 IASF attack aircraft were engaged in air strikes against targets located from Lake Kar'un to Port Sidon. F-15s and Kfir fighters of the IASF were providing combat air patrol for the attacking Israeli aircraft when Syrian MiG-21s attempted to engage the strike flights. The CAP flight took on the MiGs and, as a result, in a short but intense air battle five MiG-21s were shot down. The F-15 and IAI Kfir both claimed their first aerial victory for the IASF.

Forced by security issues the IASF for over forty years has maintained a very stringent control over photographs of its aircraft and information regarding aircrews. The IASF censors have eased restriction somewhat, but not completely. In many of the narratives presented herein the identity and rank of aircrew members may only contain a single letter. If the identity of the aircrew or information regarding a particular aircraft is censored in the source material that restriction shall be maintained, even where the information is known to the author.

F-15A Baptism of Fire
Brigadier General Melnik:

That day the squadron commander had me called out of a meeting and ordered me to report to the squadron within twenty minutes. I guessed the reason for my summons immediately. We took off with Lieutenant Colonel B., the squadron commander, flying lead, and me flying number two.

The flight of F-15s from the 'Double Tail' Squadron visually acquired eight MiGs heading directly at them. The flight was cleared to engage and cleared their aircraft to do battle with the approaching Syrian Arab Air Force MiGs. By this time the skies were full of air-to-air missiles being fired by both Israeli and Syrian aircraft.

Two MiGs positioned a little lower than Melnik passed in front of him. It was obvious from the way they were manoeuvring that they were aware of the F-15s.

Five seconds passed from the moment I identified them to the moment in which I had one in my sights. I fired an accurate missile which split the MiG in two. Barely a minute passed, and four more MiGs found themselves planted firmly in the ground.

The IASF radio traffic was full of excited pilots shouting 'hipalti!' – 'I scored a kill!'

Once on the ground and when everyone had told of their kills, Major Melnik uttered one sentence that everyone still remembers, 'Say what you will – I was the first.'

Baz No. 663 is seen in this photograph taxiing past the photographer. Painted on the fuselage of the aircraft in Hebrew is the nickname of this historic F-15, Hamadlik (Fire Igniter). Also visible on the fuselage is the MiG kill marking denoting the historic first aerial victory of No. 663's MiG-21 kill on 27 June 1979. This was the first air-to-air victory in the world for the American-built fighter but it wouldn't be the last. (O. Zidon Collection)

27 June 1979
11 June 1982

F-15B, No. 404
Hetz Mi Keshet/Arrow from Bow
Double Tail Squadron

Major Yoel Feldsho
Captain/Major Shaul Simon
Captain Amir Hodorov

Baz 404 sits in a shelter protecting IASF personnel from the blazing desert heat while they tend to this MiG killer. This aircraft's tail number was changed from 704 to 404 sometime in the mid-1980s. The F-15B MiG killer still displays proudly two MiG kill markings for kills on 27 June 1979 and 11 June 1982. In this photograph 404 wears the tail markings of the 'Twin Tail' Squadron. (O. Zidon Collection)

F-15B-16-MC 76-1524 No. 404: aircraft destroyed: 2 MiG-21s: weapon: AIM-7F Sparrow AAM/Python-3 AAMs. Major Yoel Feldsho, flying with the 'Double Tail' Squadron out of Tel-Nof Air Base on 27 June 1979, downed a Syrian MiG-21 before it could obtain a missile lock on Major Melnik. Major Feldsho was able to establish a radar lock on the MiG with a radar-guided AIM-7F Sparrow missile and launched the missile which tracked to the enemy MiG and detonated, destroying the Syrian plane.

On 11 June 1982 No. 404 claimed its second Syrian MiG-21 when Captain Shaul Simon and Captain Amir Hodorov destroyed an enemy MiG-21 Fishbed with a single Python-3 air-to-air missile. This would be the second documented aerial victory for Baz 404.

27 June 1979
13 February 1981

F-15A, No. 672
Tornado
Double Tail Squadron

Major Yoram Peled
Lieutenant Colonel Benny Zinker

F-15A-17-MC 76-1511 No: 672: aircraft destroyed: 1 MiG-21; 1 MiG-25: weapon: AIM-9G Sidewinder AAM/AIM-7F Sparrow AAM. Major Yoram Peled was on a low-level CAP mission when he downed a Syrian MiG-21 with an AIM-9G air-to-air missile. Peled had locked on to the MiG and fired just seconds before another Baz pilot was about to engage. During the short air battle 'Double Tail' Squadron F-15s claimed four Syrian MiGs.

On 13 February 1981 the 'Double Tail' Squadron CO, Lieutenant Colonel Benny Zinker, was flying as the flight leader of a combat air patrol flight tasked with protecting a photographic reconnaissance mission when they were informed by ground control that Syrian fighters were airborne, and were being vectored to intercept the Israeli RF-4 reconnaissance plane. The RF-4E mission was aborted and the crew was sent home.

Zinker was in the area of the Lebanese/Israeli border when he engaged the enemy aircraft at a range of twenty-five miles. The Baz pilot launched two AIM-7F radar missiles and was about to launch a third when he witnessed a huge explosion. At the time of the kill Lieutenant Colonel Zinker was not sure what type of aircraft he had downed. It would turn out some weeks later that it was a MiG-25P Foxbat.

27 June 1979

F-15A, No. 689
Boomerang
Double Tail Squadron

Lieutenant Colonel Eitan Ben-Eliyahu

F-15A-18-MC 76-1518 No. 689: aircraft destroyed: 1 MiG-21: weapon: 20mm cannon. Lieutenant Colonel Eitan Ben-Eliyahu locked on to a MiG-21 and was about to take the MiG out when it was shot down by a Sidewinder missile fired from another IASF F-15, piloted by Lieutenant Colonel Zinker. Fortunately, for the former commanding officer of the 'Double Tail' Squadron, a

In this rare black-and-white photograph of Baz No. 672 the double MiG killer is seen taxiing on an air base in Israel. It's clear by the blacked-out squadron emblem on the tail of the aircraft that the censor didn't want the squadron identified when the photo was taken. This historic Baz was lost in 1981 in a mid-air collision with another F-15 (684). Both pilots were killed as a result of the collision. (O. Zidon Collection)

With the nickname Boomerang in Hebrew painted on the nose of No. 689 the jet is captured in this black-and-white photograph taxiing out for a training mission. The aircraft is marked with two aerial victories. One of the roundels accounts for the MiG-21 kill of 27 June 1979 credited to Lieutenant Colonel Eitan Ben-Eliyahu; the second may very well be a squadron kill. (O. Zidon Collection)

second enemy MiG presented itself. Ben-Eliyahu locked the MiG up in his gunsight and fired a burst from the Baz's 20mm cannon which resulted in the demise of the Syrian plane.

24 September 1979
31 December 1980
9 June 1982

F-15A, No. 695
Ha Kochav / The Star
Double Tail Squadron

Major Avner Naveh
Captain Yoav Stern
Captain Oran Hampel

F-15A-18-MC 76-1521 No. 695: aircraft destroyed: 4 MiG-21s: weapons: Python-3 AAM / AIM-7F Sparrow AAMs / 20mm cannon. During September 1979 a Syrian MiG-23 Flogger launched a number of air-to-air missiles in an attempt to shot down an IASF RF-4E. The Phantom was able to fend off the Flogger attack and return home safely.

In retaliation for the aggressive action of the Syrians over Lebanon the Israelis set a trap to engage Syrian Arab AF MiGs. The IASF launched two sections of F-15s. One section was designed to lure the MiGs into action while the second flight of four Baz from the 'Double Tail' Squadron would do the interception.

The Syrians scrambled six MiG-21s and in just over a minute four were shot down by the IASF F-15s. Major Avner Naveh downed the first MiG with an air-to-air Python-3 missile. He further claimed a second MiG-21 kill with the internal 20mm cannon of the F-15.

With four Syrian Arab Air Force MiG-21 kills credited to No. 695 the MiG killer is depicted in this photograph sitting in a shelter armed with air-to-air missiles. The four kills were made from 1979 to 1982 with the last in June 1982. There is presently an F-15 Baz on display at the IASF Museum with the No. 695 and marked with four aerial victories. The museum display aircraft is not the original 695 which is still in service with the IASF. (O. Zidon Collection)

On 31 December 1980 Captain Yoav Stern claimed the third kill credited to No. 695 when he downed a Syrian MiG-21 with a Python-3 missile. The fourth kill to this F-15 was credited to Captain Oran Hampel who added a MiG-21 on 9 June 1982. Hampel brought down his MiG with the AIM-7F Sparrow missile.

24 September 1979

F-15A, No. 676
No Name Given
Double Tail Squadron

Captain Dedi Rosenthal

F-15A-17-MC 76-1513 No. 676: aircraft destroyed: 1 MiG-21: weapon: AIM-7F Sparrow AAM. Captain Dedi Rosenthal was part of the ambush flight that shot down four out of six Syrian MiG-21s on 24 September 1979. Shortly after Major Avner Naveh, the flight leader, shot down his first of two MiGs, Rosenthal locked on to an enemy MiG with a radar-guided Sparrow missile and, once all the firing parameters were satisfied, pulled the trigger launching the missile. The missile proved to be a direct hit resulting in the destruction of another SyAAF MiG.

F-15 No. 692 has been credited to date with but one aerial victory as attested to by the lone MiG kill symbol painted on its nose. Though only credited with one aerial victory 692 appears in the photograph in full alert, configured with Python-3 and AIM-120 air-to-air missiles ready to add to that total. (O. Zidon Collection)

Baz No.676 was the aircraft flown by Captain Dedi Rosenthal of the 'Double Tail' Squadron on 24 September 1979 when he shot down a MiG-21 over southern Lebanon. Just five days after the MiG-21 kill this aircraft was lost during a bad weather landing at Tel-Nof Air Base. The pilot, Guy Golan, was killed as a direct result of the crash. In this somewhat grainy black-and-white photograph, 676 was captured landing after a combat air patrol mission. The MiG killer appears in this photograph configured with air-to-air missiles. (O. Zidon Collection)

24 September 1979

F-15A, No. 692
Galaxy
Double Tail Squadron

Relik Shafir

F-15A-18-MC 76-1520 No. 92: aircraft destroyed: 1 MiG-21: weapon: AIM-9G Sidewinder AAM. The fourth MiG kill of 24 September 1979 was credited to Relik Shafir of the 'Double Tail' Squadron. The ambush that day, like the air battle of 27 June 1979, was designed by the IASF in response to the aggressive action of the Syrian Arab

Air Force over Lebanon. The defensive air operations by the IASF were intended to serve as deterrence to the Syrians over Lebanon.

24 August 1980

F-15A, No. 696
Haziz/Firecracker
Double Tail Squadron

Major Ilan Margalit

The MiG killer No. 696 is shown upon completing a training sortie. Many of the older F-15s of the Zora Ha'Avir Ve'Halal, like 696, have been upgraded giving the Baz air-to-ground capabilities, including use of JDAM and Rafael Popeye munitions. (O. Zidon Collection)

This photograph of Haziz (Firecracker) No. 696 was taken as the MiG killer was preparing to launch from what appears to be a forward operating location. The solitary MiG kill symbol on the nose of the aircraft denotes Major Ilan Margalit's aerial victory over the Syrian Arab AF pilot Nabil Girgis who managed to survive the engagement. (Y. Lapid Collection)

F-15A-18-MC 76-1522 No. 696: aircraft destroyed: 1 MiG-21: weapon: AIM-7F Sparrow AAM. On 24 August 1980 the IASF and Syrian Arab AF again engaged in air combat over Lebanon. IASF RF-4Es were conducting a photo reconnaissance mission when the Syrians launched a flight of four MiGs to intercept the reconnaissance aircraft.

The IASF combat air patrol flight tasked with protecting the RF-4Es was vectored towards the fast approaching MiG-21s.

Major Ilan Margalit visually acquired one of the MiG-21s heading directly at him. Both aircraft were on a 'collision course' when Margalit unleashed one of his AIM-7 missiles. The missile tracked directly to the target and, in an instant, the MiG-21 was seen to explode and disintegrate.

31 December 1980
9 June 1982
11 June 1982

F-15A, No. 646
Ra'am/Thunder
Double Tail Squadron

Captain Yair Rachmilevic
Captain Avi Maor
Major Ofer Lapidot

F-15A Baz 646 is seen in this photograph with the tail markings of the 'Double Tail' Squadron. No. 646 was one of the full-scale development (FSD) airframes supplied to the IASF in December 1976. Even though No. 646 is credited with four aerial victories the aircraft was not chosen to undergo the avionics upgrade programme (AUP) due to the age of the airframe. (O. Zidon Collection)

F-15A-6-MC 72-0118 No. 646: aircraft destroyed: 3 MiG-21s; 1 MiG-23: weapons: AIM-9G Sidewinder AAMs/Python-3 AAMs/20mm cannon. During November and December 1980 the IASF continued to attack PLO strongholds throughout Lebanon, particularly in the southern part of the country. On 31 December 1980 the Syrian Arab AF attempted to disrupt Israeli air operations by scrambling MiGs to intercept the IASF fighter-bombers. Captain Yair Rachmilevic was flying as part of the CAP flight protecting the strike aircraft when he identified a Syrian MiG-21. He immediately engaged the enemy aircraft by launching three Python air-to-air missiles which tracked to the MiG. This kill was the tenth for the Baz.

On 9 June 1982 Captain Avi Maor was flying Baz 646 as part of a four-plane combat air patrol flight when they intercepted two MiG-23 Floggers of the Syrian Arab Air Force. The F-15 CAP flight attacked the Floggers and downed both enemy aircraft. One of the Floggers was downed by a Python-3 launched by Maor. Maor observed the pilot in his chute shortly after the destruction of the MiG-23.

During the same mission Captain Avi Maor would claim a second MiG. Maor downed the enemy MiG with a burst from his 20mm cannon. This was the first of only two gun kills credited to IASF Baz pilots during the air battles over Lebanon.

On 11 June 1982 IASF F-15s and F-16s continued to rule the skies over Lebanon. On this date Major Ofer Lapidot claimed yet another aerial victory taking out a MiG-21 with the Python-3 air-to-air missile.

29 July 1981

F-15A, No. 673
Ha Oketz/The Sting
Double Tail Squadron

Major Shaul Simon

F-15A-17-MC 76-1512 No: 673: aircraft destroyed: 1 MiG-25: weapon: AIM-7F Sparrow AAM. On 29 July 1981 the IASF shot down a second MiG-25 that was attempting to engage an RF-4E on a reconnaissance flight over Lebanon. The Syrians scrambled two MiG-21s and two MiG-25s in an attempt to intercept the Israeli RF-4E.

The Syrian aircraft were intercepted by F-15s from the 'Double Tail' Squadron. Major Shaul Simon visually acquired the pair of Foxbats and, once in range, locked on to one of them with an AIM-7F radar air-to-air missile. Once the weapon was on its way it tracked directly to the target and, within seconds, struck the enemy MiG, totally destroying the Syrian top-end fighter before it had a chance to engage the RF-4E.

F-15 Baz No. 673 was captured in this outstanding photograph just as the aircraft touched down. The nickname in Hebrew painted on No. 673 is Ha Oketz which translates in English to 'The Sting'. The markings on the aircraft are so clear and sharp that the image is more like a work of art than a mere photo. No. 673 is proudly wearing the markings of the 'Double Tail' Squadron. Note the smiling eagle's head on the inner surface of the vertical stabilizer. (O. Zidon Collection)

7 June 1982
9 June 1982

F-15A, No. 658
Typhoon
Double Tail Squadron

Major Ofer Lapidot
Captain Gil Rapaport

F-15A-17-MC 76-1506 No. 658: aircraft destroyed: 2 MiG-23s: weapons: Python-3 AAM/AIM-7F Sparrow AAM. Major Ofer Lapidot was south of Beirut on a CAP mission when his flight was vectored to intercept a flight of Syrian aircraft that were becoming a threat to IASF strike aircraft. Lapidot visually identified an enemy MiG-23 at approximately seven miles and informed the flight that he had positively identified the target and was locked on with a Sparrow missile. The missile launched but failed to take out the MiG. Lapidot manoeuvred into Python range and at a distance of approximately one and a half miles, well within visual range (VR), fired the missile. Lapidot did not observe the missile hit the Russian-built Flogger. However, other members of his flight did see the kill and confirmed his victory.

On 9 June 1982 the Syrian Arab AF lost twenty-five aircraft to IASF fighters. The 'Double Tail' Squadron's F-15 pilots were credited with eleven of these kills. One of those eleven was accomplished by Baz pilot Captain Gil Rapaport, who downed a MiG-23 with a radar-guided Sparrow missile.

8 June 1982
10 June 1982
19 November 1985

F-15D, No. 957
Markia Shchakim/Sky Blazer
Double Tail Squadron
Spearhead Squadron

Captain Shaul Schwartz
Captain Reuven Solan

Major Avner Naveh
Captain Michael Cohen
Yuval Ben-Dor
Ofer Paz

This air superiority F-15, No. 658, was photographed at Tel-Nof Air Base during Israel's fifty-ninth Independence Day celebrations. Baz 658 claimed the first F-15 aerial victory of the Lebanon War on 7 June 1982 when Major Ofer Lapidot shot down a Syrian MiG-23. Captain Gail Rapaport of the 'Double Tail' Squadron claimed a second MiG-23 kill credited to No. 658. (T. Ben-Aim Collection)

F-15D-28-MC 80-0133 No. 957: aircraft destroyed: 2 MiG-21s; 3 MiG-23s: weapons: AIM-7F Sparrow AAMs/Python-3 AAMs. On 8 June 1982 IASF strike aircraft launched an aggressive bombing campaign directed at Syrian troop concentrations in Lebanon. The IASF air strikes on Syrian troops forced the Syrian Arab AF to generate a large number of combat sorties in an attempt to intercept the strike aircraft. F-15D pilot Captain Shaul Schwartz and his navigator Captain Reuven Solan were leading Palace flight when they were vectored by ground controllers to intercept a flight of Syrian MiGs hell-bent on attacking one of the IASF strike flights.

Palace 01 acquired the enemy aircraft and visually identified it as a MiG-21. The MiG pilot attempted to evade Palace 01 and his wingman by manoeuvring in a banking turn to the south in full afterburner. Schwartz fired a single Sparrow missile at the fleeing

enemy fighter. The missile tracked true to the target and within seconds the MiG-21 exploded, falling to the ground in flames. Schwartz's wingman also claimed and was credited with a MiG-21 victory in the same engagement.

The ground war in the Lebanon Valley grew in intensity on 10 June 1982, particularly in the area south of the Beirut-Damascus highway. Israeli and Syrian ground troops were heavily engaged, which forced the Syrian Arab Air Force to switch operations from air-to-air to air-to-ground in support of their ground forces.

IASF aircraft continued to provide combat air patrol mission for their attacking aircraft. During air operations on 10 June Major Avner Naveh and his back-seater, Captain Michael Cohen, from the Double Tail Squadron downed three Syrian MiGs. They thus became the first Baz pilots to claim three kills in the F-15 during a single interception mission. The first of their three kills involved the destruction of two MiG-23 Floggers followed by a MiG-21. Naveh's three aerial victories made him the world's first F-15 ace.

Baz 686 is seen in this photograph taxiing on the runway of an IASF air base after completing a quick reaction alert (QRA) or combat air patrol (CAP) mission. The aircraft is seen in the tail markings of the 'Double Tail' Squadron and is heavily armed with air-to-air missiles. Seen on the vertical stabilizer is an oversize IASF badge and special emblem which adorned IASF aircraft during the IASF Golden Jubilee celebrations. (O. Zidon Collection)

Baz 957 in the tail markings of the 'Spearhead' Squadron was captured moments after lift-off heading for a training sortie. The 'Spearhead' Squadron was established as the IASF's second F-15 squadron on 16 June 1982. It didn't take long for the squadron to claim its first aerial victory. On 24 June 1982 it accounted for two MiG-23 Floggers.

On 10 June 1982 Major Avner Naveh and Captain Michael Cohen flew this particular F-15 to become the first IASF crew to down three enemy aircraft in a single interception mission. Coincidentally, it established Major Avner Naveh as the first F-15 ace in the world.

During May 1983 Baz 957 was involved in a mid-air collision with an IASF A-4 Ahit in which the F-15 lost almost its entire right wing. The pilot, Captain Ziv Nadivi, and his navigator, Yehoar Gal, in an unbelievable test of airmanship were able to keep the aircraft in the air and bring it safely down at Ramon Air Base. (O. Zidon Collection)

On 19 November 1985 Yuval Ben-Dor and Ofer Paz, flying with the 'Spearhead' Squadron on a CAP mission in direct support of a reconnaissance flight over Lebanon, were vectored to intercept a flight of Syrian Floggers. During the engagement their first attempts at taking out the enemy fighters with an AIM-7 failed. The CAP flight manoeuvred into position. Once in position, Ben-Dor selected a Python-3 air-to-air missile and fired. The missile tracked directly to the target and totally destroyed the Syrian fighter.

Major Ronen Shapira claimed his MiG kill during air operations on the second day of the Lebanon War. While engaged in a CAP mission, Shapira was in the awkward position of having a MiG-21 on his tail. The Baz pilot executed a low-speed high-G turn which enabled him to manoeuvre his aircraft into the six o'clock position of the MiG, arm and fire an air-to-air missile. The missile launched but failed to hit the target. A second missile was launched (Python-3) and this time struck the MiG. (O. Zidon Collection)

8 June 1982
9 June 1982

F-15A, No. 686
Ha'Lohet/Burning Hot
Double Tail Squadron

Captain Yoram Hoffman
Major Ronen Shapira

F-15A-18-MC 76-1517 No. 686: aircraft destroyed: 2 MiG-21s: weapons: AIM-7F Sparrow AAMs/Python-3 AAMs. Captain Yoram Hoffman was flying as Palace 02 on 8 June 1982 when he located a low-flying, fast-moving target east of Beirut. He positively identified the target as being a Syrian MiG-21 Fishbed. Hoffman obtained a radar lock on the target and, after satisfying launch requirements, fired the missile. Hoffman's missile scored a direct hit on the enemy aircraft, destroying it on impact.

8 June 1982

F-15C, No. 818
Tamnoon/Octopus
Double Tail Squadron

Major Shaul Simon

F-15C-28-MC 80-0125 No. 818: aircraft destroyed: 1 MiG-23: weapon: AIM-7F Sparrow AAM. On 8 June 1982 Major Shaul Simon (Baz 818) and his wingman Debi Rosenthal (Baz 832) both engaged the same Syrian MiG-23. In the confusion of battle both pilots simultaneously locked on the Flogger and launched an AIM-7F. The evidence is not exactly clear which missile hit the MiG first and so the kill is listed as a shared victory.

8 June 1982

F-15C, No. 832
Ha Shishi Be Yuni/The Sixth of June
Double Tail Squadron

Captain Dedi Rosenthal

No. 818 is shown parked in the hot sun fully configured with Sparrow and Python-3 AAMs. In the photograph 818 is clearly marked with two aerial victories. Several sources claim that the aircraft has been erroneously marked for years as a double MiG killer. The same sources state that this aircraft only has to its credit a half kill, and shares the other half with Baz 832. (O. Zidon Collection)

F-15C-29-MC 80-0128 No. 832: aircraft destroyed: 1 MiG-23: weapon: AIM-7F Sparrow AAM. It was Captain Dedi Rosenthal's AIM-7F Sparrow missile which claimed the second half of the 8 June 1982 kill of a Syrian MiG-23. When the engagement took place Rosenthal was flying on the wing of Major Shaul Simon. The pair had separated from their four-plane flight when the kill was made.

9 June 1982

F-15C, No. 684
Ha Raped/The Vampire
Double Tail Squadron

Major Ronen Shapira
Major Yoram Peled

F-15C-18-MC 76-1516 No. 684: aircraft destroyed: 1 MiG-23; 1 MiG-21: weapons: AIM-7F Sparrow AAM; Python-3 AAM. The MiG-23 was in full afterburner to the east of Major Ronen Shapira when he visually acquired and identified the enemy jet. Shapira obtained a radar lock-on and at approximately 1,500 metres fired a Sparrow missile which tracked and hit the Syrian MiG. The MiG was seen to explode into a huge fireball.

Major Yoram Peled flew No. 684 on the afternoon combat air patrol (CAP) mission from Tel-Nof Air Base and, like Shapira,

Baz 832 appears in this close-up colour photograph on static display during an IASF air show. Now assigned to the 'Spearhead' Squadron the aircraft is marked with one and half Syrian Arab Air Force roundels, adding to the confusion of just how many kills this F-15 and Baz 818 actually have. In Shlomo Aloni's book Israeli F-15 Eagle Units in Combat *there is a similar photograph of 818 marked with one and a half kills. (O. Zidon Collection)*

The Vampire, Baz 684, appears in this black-and-white photograph heavily armed with AIM-7 Sparrow air-to-air missiles and Python-3 air-to-air missiles tucked under the wings. Having served with the IASF for some time this aircraft was lost in a mid-air collision on 15 August 1988. Baz 684 was named Ha Raped (Vampire) when the F-15C claimed two MiG kills during 9 June 1982. Why the aircraft is marked with three kill markings is unknown. The third may be a squadron kill. No. 684 is seen in the second photograph taxiing past the camera. (O. Zidon Collection)

claimed a kill of a Syrian MiG-21. Peled was leading a four-plane flight of F-15s when they crossed a mountain ridge and entered the Lebanon Valley. The flight became engaged with a flight of Syrian fighters and, during the ensuing air battle, downed a number of enemy MiGs. One MiG-21 was credited to Peled who at the time of his aerial victory was flying Baz 684. The Fishbed was shot down with a Python-3 air-to-air missile.

9 June 1982
10 June 1982

F-15C, No. 802
Panther
Double Tail Squadron

Lieutenant Colonel Moshe Melnik
Captain Noam Knaani

F-15C-27-MC 80-0122 No. 802: aircraft destroyed: 3 MiG-23s; 1 MiG-21: weapons: AIM-7F Sparrow AAMs; Python-3 AAMs. On 9 June 1982 Lieutenant Colonel Moshe Melnik was leading a four-plane combat air patrol flight when they engaged, fired on and downed four Syrian aircraft. Melnik locked on to a Russian-built Flogger with a radar-guided air-to-air missile and the weapon hit the target, destroying the MiG-23. After the engagement the

One of only three F-15s of the IASF to be credited with four aerial victories, Baz 802 appears in this in-flight photograph in formation with another F-15. While assigned to the 'Spearhead' Squadron in May 1994 No. 802 was heavily damaged during a landing accident at Tel-Nof Air Base. Panther (Hebrew nickname) was repaired and continues to fly with the IASF.

The second photograph of 802 provides a close-up view of the Python air-to-air missile. The blue colour indicates that this particular missile is an inert training weapon. In the photo 802 still wears the name Panther and the four kill markings of Melnik and Knaani during the Lebanon War. (O. Zidon / T. Ben-Aim Collections)

four F-15s returned to their CAP mission where the flight again encountered a pair of MiG-21s. The MiGs were able to launch a number of AAMs at the IASF F-15s but, fortunately for the Israeli pilots, the Syrian missiles failed to hit their targets. Seizing on the opportunity, Melnik engaged one of the Fishbeds and launched a Python-3 which tracked true to the target. While he was thus engaged, Melnik's wingman, Captain Avi Maor, shot down the second MiG with his 20mm internal cannon.

Captain Noam Knaani from the 'Double Tail' Squadron was flying Baz 802 the day after Melnik claimed the two Syrian MiGs while flying Baz 802. Knaani was on a CAP mission when he engaged, fired on and destroyed two of the enemy MiG-23s. Knaani's weapon was the Python-3 air-to-air missile.

10 June 1982
F-15C, No. 848
Nesher / Eagle
Double Tail Squadron

Captain Yoram Hoffman
Captain Ziv Nadivi

F-15C-29-MC 80-0130 No. 848: aircraft destroyed: 1 MiG-21; 1 Gazelle: weapons: 20mm cannon; Python-3 AAM. F-15 Baz pilot Captain Yoram Hoffman of the 'Double Tail' Squadron claimed his second F-15 aerial victory flying the F-15 named Nesher (Eagle) downing a Syrian MiG-21 with 20mm cannonfire. This was one of only two cannon kills during the Lebanon War.

Captain Ziv Nadivi was credited with the only non-fixed wing kill of the Lebanon War when, on 10 June 1982, he was able to gain a position of advantage on a low and slow-flying Syrian Gazelle helicopter. Once he had the enemy chopper locked up he launched one Python-3 which tracked to the target. The Gazelle was destroyed in the explosion.

10 June 1982
11 June 1982
19 November 1985

F-15C, No. 840
Commando
Double Tail Squadron
Spearhead Squadron

Lieutenant Colonel Benny Zinker
Lieutenant Colonel Yiftach Shadmi
Major Avner Naveh

F-15C-29-MC 80-0129 No. 840: aircraft destroyed: 3 MiG-23s; 1 MiG-21: weapons: Python-3 AAMs; 20mm cannon. Lieutenant Colonel Benny Zinker claimed his first MiG kill as an F-15 driver on 13 February 1981 when he became the first pilot in history to take out a Russian-built MiG-25 Foxbat with the AIM-7F Sparrow radar missile. He added to his tally on 10 June 1982 when he destroyed a Syrian MiG-23 with a Python-3 air-to-air missile.

On 11 June 1982 the Israeli and Syrian governments agreed to a ceasefire. However, before the ceasefire took effect the IASF would

No. 848, nickname Nesher (Eagle), was photographed during its arrival at Tel-Nof Air Base. The MiG killer 848 appears in a clean condition in this photograph which may suggest the pilot had just completed a training sortie. In this post-Lebanon War photograph the 'Double Tail' Squadron front-line fighter is still wearing the two Syrian roundels proclaiming its two kills on 10 June 1982. (O. Zidon Collection)

'Spearhead' Squadron F-15s flown by Major Avner Naveh, Yuval Ben Dor and Ofer Paz were operating with a flight of F-16s on 19 November 1985 when the Syrian Arab Air Force launched a flight of MiG-23s to intercept the IASF aircraft. Major Avner Naveh, who by 1985 had become the Commanding Officer (CO) of the 'Spearhead' Squadron, and his flight were vectored by ground control to engage the Floggers. The flight initially engaged the Syrians with AIM-7F Sparrow missiles, all of which failed. Switching to the Python-3, Naveh downed two of the MiG-23s, bringing his tally of Baz kills to six and a half.

For many years Baz No. 840 was credited and marked with six aerial victories. It's known that the aircraft downed four Syrian MiGs during combat service with the IASF. In these two photographs 840 is clearly marked with the six Syrian roundels on the fuselage below the canopy. Later research showed that the aircraft could claim only four aerial victories.

In the profile shot of Baz 840 the markings of the 'Spearhead' Squadron are carried on the inner surface of the vertical stabilizers. It has been suggested by some sources that the two extra kill markings were added to No. 840 before the MiG killer was transferred from the 'Double Tail' Squadron and represent two non-weapon kills credited to the 'Double Tail' Squadron during the Lebanon War. In any event, in 2001, the two extra roundels were removed and 840 now reflects just four kills.

claim an additional five Syrian Arab AF MiGs. One of the last five kills of the 1982 Lebanon War was achieved by Lieutenant Colonel Yiftach Shadmi from the 'Double Tail' Squadron who, whilst on a CAP mission, destroyed a MiG-21 with 20mm cannon-fire. Of the thirty-three kills credited to the Baz during the war only two were by the gun.

Baz 840 appears in this close-up photo taken in 1993 still marked with the six kills. It also appears that 840 may be armed with live air-to-air missiles. Training or inert missiles are, as a rule, blue. (O. Zidon / T. Ben-Ami Collections)

10 June 1982

F-15C, No. 828
O'ach/Eagle Owl
Double Tail Squadron

Captain Gil Rapaport

F-15C-28-MC 80-0127 No. 828: aircraft destroyed: 1 MiG-23: weapon: Python-3 air-to-air missile (AAM). During the first days of the Lebanon War IASF aircraft involved in Operation ARTVAZ (Mole Cricket) attacked and destroyed numerous Syrian surface-to-air missile sites. Flying combat air patrol for the strike aircraft involved in the suppression of enemy air defences (SEAD) were F-15s from the 'Double Tail' Squadron. During one such CAP mission Captain Gil Rapaport aligned himself behind a Syrian MiG-21 and, once in range, launched a Python-3 which tracked directly to the MiG and, upon impact, exploded, destroying it.

10 June 1982

F-15B, No. 408
Merkevet Esh (Chariot of Fire)
Double Tail Squadron

Captain Shaul Schwartz
Uzi Shapira

F-15B-16-MC 76-1525 No. 408: aircraft destroyed: 1 MiG-21: weapon: Python-3 AAM. Captain Shaul Schwartz was the pilot of Baz 708 (later 408) when he claimed his second MiG kill of the war. Schwartz and his navigator, Uzi Shapira, were flying as part of a combat air patrol formation over the Lebanon Valley when they engaged and destroyed a MiG-21 with a Python-3 air-to-air missile.

10 June 1982

F-15D, No. 455
Roach Partzim/Stormy Wind
Double Tail Squadron

Major Mickey Lev

When Baz No. 828 claimed its kill on 10 June 1982 Captain Gil Rapaport and his MiG killer were assigned to the 'Double Tail' Squadron. In this photograph 828 is in the post-war markings of the 'Spearhead' Squadron. Named Eagle Owl, 828 is depicted climbing in a full afterburner take-off. Silhouetted against the blue sky the sleek lines and impressive afterburner flame are clearly evident and demonstrate the brute force of the F-15. (O. Zidon Collection)

On 10 June 1982 when Schwartz and Shapira claimed their MiG-21, their aircraft's number was 708. On most, if not all F-15s with the prefix digit '7', that digit was replaced with a '4.' In this photograph Baz 408 is still assigned to the 'Double Tail' Squadron, and still decorated with the kill marking crediting Schwartz and Shapira with their MiG-21 kill. (O. Zidon Collection)

No. 408, nickname Chariot of Fire (Merkevet Esh), is shown in this colour photograph returning from a training mission, which is evident by its clean configuration. (S. Williams Collection)

F-15D-27-MC 80-0132 No. 455: aircraft destroyed: 1 MiG-21: weapon: Python-3 AAM. Major Mickey Lev was flying in a four-plane combat air patrol flight on 10 June 1982 when he tangled with a Syrian MiG-21 over the Lebanon Valley. The IASF pilot was able to identify visually the enemy aircraft as a MiG-21. The Syrian plane was well within range of the Python-3 air-to-air missile and, once a good tone was established, he fired the weapon. The missile was seen to fly to the target and detonate, destroying the MiG. Lev failed to pull away from the target quickly enough and, as a result, flew through the debris field of the exploding MiG causing damage to his aircraft. The Baz remained flyable and he made it home safely.

10 June 1982
24 June 1982

F-15D, No. 979
Mashak Knafaim / Wings Wave
Double Tail Squadron
Spearhead Squadron

Major Yoram Peled
Major Zvi Lipsitz

Major Yoel Feldsho
Major Zvi Lipsitz

When Lev flew his MiG kill mission the tail number of the aircraft was 955. On being transferred to the 'Double Tail' Squadron the prefix was changed to '4.' Even though this aircraft is a two-seat D model, Lev was alone in the aircraft on 10 June when he claimed his MiG.

No. 455 appears in this colour photograph landing safely, still in the markings of the 'Double Tail' Squadron. Painted on the fuselage under the cockpit are two kill markings although the aircraft was only credited with one MiG kill during the Lebanon War. The second roundel identifies this Baz as being one of the F-15s that participated in Operation WOODEN LEG, a well-co-ordinated air strike against the PLO HQ in Tunis on 1 October 1985. This operation proved again that the F-15 is truly a multi-role aircraft. (O. Zidon Collection)

F-15D-28-MC 80-0136 No. 979: aircraft destroyed: 1 MiG-21; 2 MiG-23s: weapon: Python-3 AAMs. Baz 979 was the last of the Peace Fox III F-15Ds sent to the IASF. Bearing the nickname 'Wings Wave', No. 979 was flown by Major Yoram Peled and Major Zvi Lipsitz on 10 June 1982 when they downed a Syrian MiG-21 with a Python-3 missile. Of the thirty-three aerial victories credited to the F-15 during the Lebanon War nineteen were accomplished with the Python-3. Approximately two weeks later Major Zvi Lipsitz was again in the back seat of 979 when he and Major Yoel Feldsho downed two MiG-23 Floggers.

The ceasefire of 11 June 1982 didn't end the fighting in Lebanon. In fact it continued well into August 1982. The IASF continued air operations, attacking targets throughout Lebanon pretty much unopposed by the Syrian Arab Air Force.

The Syrians did, however, send MiG-23s against the IASF on 24 June 1982. Major Yoel Feldsho and his navigator, Major Zvi Lipsitz, were leading a CAP flight (call sign Hot) when they were vectored by ground control to intercept the MiGs over Baalbeck. Feldsho acquired the MiGs over Rayak, in enemy controlled territory. At approximately 800 metres from the target he launched a Python-3 which killed the first of two MiGs.

The triple MiG killer Baz No. 979 touches down after completing its mission. In the markings of the 'Spearhead' Squadron the F-15 (nickname Wings Wave) still displays proudly the three kill markings from the Lebanon War. Some sources claim that the 10- to 12 G turn put on 979 by Feldsho and Lipsitz during the double kill on 24 June 1982 left the airframe twisted and that it remains so to this day. (O. Zidon Collection)

Shortly after engaging and downing the first Flogger, Hot leader engaged the second enemy MiG. Pulling into a 10 to 12G turn Feldsho and Lipsitz were able to obtain a position of advantage to fire a second Python-3 air-to-air missile which, like the first, found its mark, destroying the Syrian MiG.

10 June 1982

F-15A, No. 667
Tzikion/Cyclone
Double Tail Squadron

Lieutenant Colonel Yiftach Shadmi

F-15A-17-MC 76-1509 No. 667: aircraft destroyed: 1 MiG-21: weapon: Python-3 AAM. Another of the 'Double Tail' Squadron's kills of 10 June 1982 was accomplished by Lieutenant Colonel Yiftach Shadmi who, at the time of his MiG encounter, was flying on the wing of Major Yoram Peled and Major Zvi Lipsitz when each of them shot down a Syrian MiG-23. The Syrian Arab Air Force not only scrambled the two Floggers on the 10th, but also a pair of MiG-21s. While Peled and Lipsitz were heavily engaged with the flight of MiG-23s, Shadmi went after one of the MiG-21s which he easily despatched with a Python-3 air-to-air missile.

Baz No. 667 is presented in this photograph in a hardened shelter while assigned to the 'Double Tail' Squadron. The Hebrew printing on the nose of this MiG killer is the aircraft's nickname which translates as 'Cyclone'. The roundel painted on the nose stands in testament to the 10 June 1982 MiG-21 kill by Lieutenant Colonel Yiftach Shadmi. (O. Zidon Collection)

11 June 1982

F-15A, No. 678
Ha Yo'reh/The Shooter
Double Tail Squadron

Major Yoram Peled

F-15A-17-MC 76-1514 No. 678: aircraft destroyed: 2 MiG-23s: weapon: AIM-7F Sparrow AAMs. Major Yoram Peled was flying lead in Adulthood flight on a CAP mission when Syrian aircraft

The double MiG killer Baz 678 stands on a five-minute alert secured within a hardened shelter at the home of the 'Double Tail' Squadron, Tel-Nof Air Base. If forced to scramble this F-15 is configured with the new Python-4 air-to-air missile and will present a formidable adversary for any intruder. The F-15 Baz continues to be the main air superiority fighter of the Zroa Ha'Avir Ve'Halalal. (O. Zidon Collection)

were discovered operating over Rayak. Being vectored toward the formation of enemy aircraft Adulthood flight acquired the aircraft and positively identified them as MiG-23s.

Peled was able to manoeuvre to within a few miles of the trailing MiG and launch a radar-guided missile in a look-down-shoot-down mode. The missile tracked beautifully and quickly struck the aft section of the Flogger. Without hesitation Peled re-acquired the lead MiG and readied a second Sparrow for launch. Once locked on, the missile was fired and, like the first missile, tracked to the MiG. The resulting impact and explosion destroyed the lead enemy MiG.

31 August 1982

F-15C, No. 821
Peres/Lammergeyer
Spearhead Squadron

Captain Shaul Schwartz

F-15C-27-MC 80-0126 No. 821: aircraft destroyed: 1 MiG-25: weapon: AIM-7F Sparrow AAM. The Russian-piloted MiG-25RB Foxbats were able to overfly Lebanon on photo reconnaissance missions virtually untouched by IASF aircraft. The Israelis devised a plan to ambush the MiG-25 (codename Nestling) on its next reconnaissance flight.

On 31 August 1982 the Israelis set the ambush into motion when they discovered a high-flying fast-moving Nestling over Beirut. The Israelis had positioned a Hawk missile battery to engage the MiG-25 and, once locked on, it fired two Hawk surface-to-air missiles. The missiles exploded in close proximity to the fast-

No. 821 flown by Captain Shaul Schwartz on the 31 August 1982 mission is seen in this April 1982 photograph being turned over to aircraft maintainers at Tel-Nof Air Base. In this black-and-white photograph Baz 821 wears the Hebrew name Peres (Lammergeyer, a large old world vulture that in flight resembles a huge falcon). This aircraft was lost in a training accident on 10 February 1991 in which the pilot, Israel Ornan, was killed. (A. Dor Collection)

moving Foxbat. The explosion damaged the MiG-25 and, trailing black smoke, it was picked up by an IASF F-15 Baz. Captain Shaul Schwartz locked on to the descending MiG with an AIM-7F Sparrow missile and quickly finished off the MIG.

The official records credits Schwartz and the Hawk missile battery with a shared kill for the 31 August 1982 shooting down of the MiG-25RB Foxbat.

Lebanon 1982 to Tunis 1985

In just a few days in June 1982 the IASF, flying American F-15 Bazs and F-16 Sparrowhawks, totally destroyed the entire Russian designed and supplied air-defence system in Lebanon. The IASF destroyed in aerial combat over eighty Syrian aircraft without a single loss. If that wasn't enough the IASF was able to take out the Syrian surface-to-air missile systems almost at will. The poor performance of the best of Russian weapons systems sent the generals in Russia into a panic. The demoralized Russians blamed the failure of the poor performance on the Syrian military.

Mivtza REGEL ETZ/Operation WOODEN LEG

On 25 September 1985 a group of Palestine Liberation Organization (PLO) terrorists killed three unarmed Israeli civilians who were holidaying on their yacht off Larnaca, Cyprus. Credit for this cowardly act was claimed by Force 17, a section within the PLO.

In response to a recent rocket attack into a settlement in northern Israel and the unprovoked murder of the three Israeli civilians, the Israeli government voted to approve a retaliatory air strike against the PLO.

On 1 October 1985 the IASF launched Operation REGEL ETZ (WOODEN LEG) from Tel Nof Air Base against the PLO headquarters in Hammam al-Shatt, Tunisia, about twelve miles from the capital, Tunis. The mission would prove to be the longest air strike that the IASF had undertaken since Entebbe in 1976 and it's believed that the mission was the first time that the F-15 Baz was used as a strike fighter. The strike aircraft would have to fly more than 1,280 miles over water. In order to accomplish the long-range mission two modified Boeing 707 tankers from the 'Desert Giant' Squadron would meet the strike aircraft in mid-flight over the Mediterranean Sea. Having rendezvoused with the two

Boeing 707 tankers and completed the in-flight refuelling phase the two flights of Bazs would continue on their designed flight profile, avoiding detection by Egyptian and Libyan radar and US Navy vessels deployed in the Mediterranean. The operational aspects of the mission would be directed and controlled by highly experienced command personnel flying in a specially equipped Boeing 707 airborne command post.

The aircraft selected by the IASF to deliver the blow to the terrorists were the F-15B/D Bazs of the 'Spearhead' Squadron. Having proven itself in the Lebanon War as an interceptor the F-15 would now prove itself as an effective bomber. It has long been accepted that the Heyl Ha'Avir were the first to deploy the F-15 Baz in the strike aircraft role. The aircraft and pilots were handpicked and GBU-15-weapons-qualified for the mission. The actual air strike on the target was to be carried out by two strike flights of F-15s armed with unpowered GBU-15 glide weapons.

The first six F-15s to hit the seaside PLO headquarters were assigned to deliver GBU-15s on their designated targets. The GBU-15 is an unpowered glide weapon used to destroy high value targets. This highly manoeuvrable weapon has an optimal, low-to-medium altitude delivery capability with pinpoint accuracy. The last two F-15s over the target were both armed with unguided general-purpose (GP) Mk 82 500lb bombs.

After refuelling somewhere between Crete and Italy the strike force picked up the Tunisian coastline and set Operation WOODEN LEG in motion.

As a direct result of the air strike, which was accomplished in six minutes, the IASF aircraft destroyed almost the entire PLO complex, including the PLO chairman's bureau and the headquarters of Force 17. Between sixty and a hundred terrorists were killed while another seventy were wounded.

F-15 Bazs of WOODEN LEG

The following F-15 photographs are of Zroa Ha'Avir Ve'Halalal aircraft that are known to have taken part in the 1 October 1985 air strike against the PLO headquarters in Tunis. The identity of the pilots and navigators will not be disclosed, nor the numbers of the squadrons to which the aircraft belonged. Squadrons will be only identified by the name of the squadron.

1 October 1985

F-15D, No. 280
Yad Ha Nefetz/Shutter Hand
Spearhead Squadron

Classified
Classified

Baz 280 is captured in this colour photograph lifting off from Tel-Nof Air Base. The aircraft is pictured in the tail markings of the 'Double Tail' Squadron. Painted on the fuselage by the name of the aircraft is a special emblem (a roundel with a GBU-15 bomb) to denote the 1 October 1985 Tunis raid. No. 280 is one of the strike aircraft credited with a direct hit on its target with the GBU-15. (O. Zidon Collection)

F-15D-35-MC 83-0064 No. 280: Target: PLO headquarters: weapon: GBU-15 glide bombs. The two-seater F-15D Baz 280 was one of the aircraft chosen to participate in the Tunis Raid and was armed with GBU-15 glide bombs. The attacking IASF jets caught terrorists totally off guard and the aircraft were able to place their weapons on the target with great effect.

1 October 1985

F-15D, No. 450
Cherev Pipiyot/Two Edged Sword
Spearhead Squadron

Classified
Classified

F-15D-27-MC 80-0131 No. 450: Target: PLO headquarters: weapon: GBU-15 glide bomb. During the WOODEN LEG operation Baz 450 was one of the six strike aircraft armed with the GBU-15s used to destroy the PLO complex. Unfortunately, No. 450 returned home six hours later, having failed to drop its bombs. The crew of Baz 450 was unable to deliver their ordnance on the target because the aircraft experienced a technical malfunction of its bomb delivery system.

1 October 1985

F-15D, No. 455
Roach Partzim/Stormy Wind
Spearhead Squadron

Classified
Classified

The hostile appearance of the landscape in the background gives the impression that IASF F-15 No. 450 is taking off from another planet. This particular Baz was unable to deliver its GBU-15s on the target during Operation WOODEN LEG. The operation, however, proved that the IASF was very capable of reaching out to attack the PLO and other terrorists. (O. Zidon Collection)

F-15D-27-MC 80-0132 No. 455: Target: PLO headquarters: weapon: GBU-15 glide bomb. When IASF aircraft flew the Operation WOODEN LEG mission all national and unit markings were removed from the aircraft. F-15D No. 455 was another of the bomb-laden F-15s credited with direct hits on the PLO complex which killed sixty to one hundred of the terrorists with their GBU-15 glide bombs.

(See 10 June 1982 F-15D No. 455 for photograph.)

1 October 1985

F-15D, No. 970
Ayelet Hashachar/Morning Star
Spearhead Squadron

Classified
Classified

F-15D-28-MC 80-0135 No. 970: Target: PLO headquarters: weapon: GBU-15 glide bomb. The attack on 1 October 1985 against the PLO headquarters in Tunisia demonstrated the long-range capabilities of the IASF F-15s. This F-15D was one of the attackers and was able to place its GBU-15 glide bombs directly on target during the operation. Throughout the mission the IASF aircraft went unchallenged by the Tunisian and Syrian Arab Air Forces. The attack was such a surprise that the IASF aircraft weren't even challenged by anti-aircraft defences from within the complex.

Touch down! While Baz 970 returns safely home, another F-15 is seen in the background ready to launch. Because of the present state of the Middle East, IASF aircraft are continually flying training or 'real world' combat missions daily. The IASF maintains aircraft on a constant state of alert to respond to any aggressive act towards the State of Israel. During the mission of 1 October 1985 No. 970 flew on the wing of the leader of the WOODEN LEG operation. (O. Zidon Collection)

Utilizing brute force during this take-off shot No. 530 was captured in a full afterburner take-off. This particular photograph was taken in August 2005 when No. 530 was taking part in the first full-scale FLYING DRAGON squadron exercise in the skies over Ovda. (O. Zidon Collection)

1 October 1985

F-15C, No. 530
Chetz/Arrow
Spearhead Squadron

Classified

F-15C-36-MC 83-0057 No. 530: Target: PLO headquarters: weapon: GP free-fall 'iron' bombs. Baz 530 was one of the two single-seat D-model F-15s that flew during the historic WOODEN LEG operation. The two D models were the seventh and eighth aircraft to deliver their ordnance on the PLO complex in Tunisia. Both F-15s released their six 500lb Mk-82 bombs carried under the belly of the aircraft.

Chapter Seven

Enter the F-16A/B Netz (Sparrowhawk)

The F-16/A/B models entered service with the IASF 'First Jet' Squadron approximately four years after the F-15s entered service with the 'Double Tail' Squadron. Known as the F-16 Falcon or Viper in the United States and NATO air forces, the F-16 became known in the Zroa Ha'Avir Ve'Halalal as the Netz (Sparrowhawk).

Originally designed as a lightweight fighter the F-16 in service with the IASF quickly evolved into a true multi-role aircraft, equally capable of air-to-air or air-to-ground missions.

The first seventy-five F-16 Netzes appeared in the IASF in July of 1980 joining the 'First Jet' Squadron. The second squadron, 'Knights of the North', arrived in September 1980. Both of these squadrons were operating out of Ramat David Air Base, located near the Syrian and Lebanese borders.

The two single signature events that defined the F-16 Netz as a true multi-role fighter would be, without a doubt, the most publicized combat missions of the F-16s. The first was the air strike on 7 June 1981 that took out the 'jewel in the crown' of President Saddam Hussein's nuclear programme. Eight F-16s from the 'First Jet' and the 'Knights of the North' Squadrons flew from Etzion Air Base to the nuclear reactor at Al Tuwaitha located 10.5 miles from Baghdad, delivered their ordnance on target, destroying the nuclear reactor, and returned home safely.

The second event would have to be the performance in the Lebanon War in 1982 when the F-16s and F-4Es were tasked with the destruction of the entire Soviet-designed Syrian air defence system. Within just a matter of hours the IASF, led by the F-16s, totally devastated the surface-to-air missile systems without a single aircraft loss. Seventeen of nineteen surface-to-air missile batteries of the Syrians were destroyed during the first day. The IASF Netzes also demonstrated their air-to-air capabilities by downing approximately twenty-nine Syrian MiG-21s and 23s during the first day's air combat over the Beqaa Valley. The F-16A Netzes have accumulated to date a total of forty-seven aerial combat victories while serving with the Israeli Air and Space Force. With tension again building in the Middle East the probability is great that the F-16s of the IASF will again add to the enduring legacy of the aircraft.

The F-16 Netz, like the F-15 Baz, claimed its first aerial combat victory while engaged in the skies of the Middle East. The first kill was achieved by Rafi Raz on 28 April 1981 when he downed a Syrian Mi-8 helicopter with the internal 20mm cannon of his F-16. On 14 July 1981 Amir Nahumi downed the first fixed-wing aircraft when he engaged, fired on and destroyed a Syrian Arab AF MiG-21. The Netzes of the IASF would not claim another aerial combat victory until 1 April 1982 when Ze'ev Raz destroyed a Syrian MiG-23 Flogger.

In the following narratives information regarding particular F-16 aircrews, weapons and squadrons is somewhat limited. In some cases the pilot may only be mentioned by first name, or a single letter and no rank will be provided unless it's in the public domain. Units or squadrons will not be mentioned by squadron numbers, but referred to only by the squadron name.

Chapter Eight

F-16 Netz over Lebanon

Whoever Fires First Wins!

The IASF F-16A/B Netz, besides proving itself quite capable of flying air-to-ground missions against airfields, surface-to-air missile sites, radar sites, troop concentrations, armoured vehicles, command and control centres, communication centres etc., has amassed quite an impressive air-to-air combat record. In the skies over Lebanon during 1981–82 the F-16s claimed over forty aerial victories against Syrian Arab Air Force fighters. What follows in this chapter are photographs of IASF F-16 Netzes that have been identified and credited with Syrian Arab AF kills.

In the Lebanon War, it was not only the personal qualities of the Israeli pilots involved in the accumulated aerial combat victories that led to the one-sided victory, but the old fighter pilot adage that 'whoever fires first wins'.

28 April 1981

F-16A, No. 126
First Jet Squadron, IASF

Dubi Yoffe

F-16A-Block 5 78-0321 No. 126: aircraft destroyed: 1 Mi-8: weapon AIM-9L Sidewinder. The 'First Jet' Squadron's F-16A Netz No. 126 was flown by Dubi Yoffe on 28 April 1981 when he claimed the second Mi-8 kill in the area of Jebel Snin.

28 April 1981

F-16A, No. 112
Ra'am/Thunder
First Jet Squadron, IASF

Major Rafi Berkovich
Itzhak Gat

F-16A Netz No. 126 is shown in a full afterburner take-off into a clear blue Middle Eastern sky. Netz 126's tail markings indicate that it is now assigned to the 'Flying Wing' Squadron of the IASF. However, on 28 April 1981, this aircraft was deployed with the 'First Jet' Squadron when it was credited with the downing of a Syrian Mi-8 helicopter with a single AIM-9L Sidewinder air-to-air missile. (O. Zidon Collection)

F-16A-Block 5 78-0314 No. 112: aircraft destroyed: 1 Mi-8; 1 DR-3 Drone: weapons: M61 Vulcan 20mm cannon; AIM-9 Sidewinder air-to-air missile. 'We suddenly heard an earsplitting siren wail. We ran like madmen to our planes, revved them up and took off.'

The flight of F-16s had been scrambled to investigate Syrian helicopters operating in the area of Jebel Snin. Approximately ten miles from Riak airfield, shortly after take-off, Major Berkovich established radar contact with an unidentified aircraft. The rules of

With aerial kill markings painted on its nose, No. 112 is depicted in this photograph in full afterburner take-off from Ovda Air Base. Ovda Air Base is said to be in a great location for an active military training base. The aircraft appears with the new 'Flying Wing' Squadron emblem painted on the tail. (O. Zidon Collection)

F-16A No. 112 is seen in this undated in-flight colour photograph in formation with two other F-16s from the 'First Jet' Squadron. No. 112 has been identified as being the F-16 Netz flown by Major Rafi on 28 April 1981 when he downed a Syrian Arab AF Mi-8, establishing the first F-16 aerial victory in history. (A. Hershko Collection)

engagement required that the target be identified positively before permission was granted to engage. While waiting for permission to launch Major Berkovich lost his radar lock on the unidentified aircraft.

A short time passed before Rafi Berkovich re-acquired the target on radar and was then authorized to engage. At minimum missile range Berkovich launched an air-to-air missile at the target.

The missile left the plane on the left side with a whoosh, and I followed it with my glance. It veered downward, hit the ground and entered a small shack, and sent it up in the air.

Later that day, the announcer on the news said that 'our forces had fired rockets in the area'. Well, those so-called rockets were my misguided missile and nothing else.

Rafi Berkovich switched to cannon sights and went after the helicopter in a diving attack. Pulling in on the six o'clock position of the target, he fired. The helicopter was seen trailing a heavy black smoke trail before crashing. (IASF Official website)

In the second photograph No. 219 stands ready to respond to any would-be enemy intruder that may enter foolhardily into Israeli airspace. The aircraft is configured with four Sidewinder air-to-air missiles. The 'Golden Eagle' Squadron, like many other squadrons, maintains aircraft in hardened shelters all over Israel. (O. Zidon Collection)

Netz No. 219 was flown by the 'Knights of the North' on 14 July 1981 when Amir Nahumi downed a Syrian Arab AF MiG-21. This photograph may have been taken at Nevatim. Seen nestled in the wing root is the internal 20mm M61 Vulcan cannon. In this photograph Netz 219 has been re-assigned to the 'Golden Eagle' Squadron, the first IASF squadron to introduce the new tail art that now appears on many IASF jets. (A. Dor Collection)

14 July 1981

F-16A, No. 219
Knights of the North Squadron, IASF

Amir Nahumi

F-16A-Block 10 78-0326 No. 219: aircraft destroyed: 1 MiG-21: weapon: AIM-9L Sidewinder. The summer of 1981 was a time of heightened tension between Israelis and Syrians as the latter had been detected moving troops into the Jebel Snin area. On 14 July 1981 Amir Nahumi of the 'Knights of the North' claimed the first fixed-wing aerial victory for the F-16 when he engaged, fired on and destroyed a Syrian Arab AF MiG-21. Now a retired Brigadier General, Amir Nahumi amassed quite a combat record during his service with the IASF. The General downed four Syrian MiG-17s on his very first combat mission while an F-4 pilot and went on

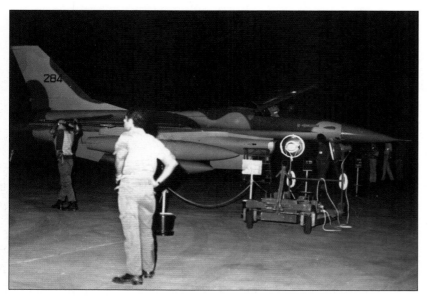

Prior to his MiG kill of 21 April 1982 Hagai Katz was already an accomplished fighter pilot, having participated in the historic 7 June 1981 air strike against the Iraqi nuclear reactor during Operation OPERA. During that operation Katz flew in Eshkol flight as Eshkol 04. The MiG killer No. 284 appears in this black-and-white nighttime photograph being prepared for a night launch. (R. Weiss Collection)

to claim four additional MiGs in the Phantom. In 1982 he would claim five more kills in the F-16 making him the first F-16 Netz ace in history.

21 April 1982

F-16A, No. 284
Negev Squadron, IASF

Hagai Katz

F-16A-Block 10D 80-0661 No. 284: aircraft destroyed: 1 MiG-23: weapon: AIM-9L Sidewinder missile-to-air missile.

21 April 1982
11 June 1982

F-16A, No. 107
Sufa (Gale Storm)
First Jet Squadron, IASF
Flying Wing Squadron, IASF

Ze'ef Ra
Eliezer Shkedi
Eytan Stibbe

F-16A-Block 5 78-0311 No. 107: aircraft destroyed: 4 MiG-23s; 1 Su-22; 1 SA.342L Gazelle: weapons: AIM-9L Sidewinder AAMs; 20mm M61 Vulcan cannon. On 1 April 1982 Ze'ev Raz of the 'First Jet' Squadron was the first to claim an aerial victory in F-16A Netz

No. 107 when he downed a Syrian Arab AF MiG-23 Flogger. This particular jet would go into combat again on 11 June 1982 during the Lebanon War and be credited with five and a half additional kills, which established No. 107 as the leading F-16 MiG killer in the world.

On 11 June 1982 an IASF pilot, Eliezer Shkedi of the 'Flying Wing' Squadron, claimed four aerial victories in one mission. Shkedi downed two MiG-23s, one Su-22 and one Gazelle. The Netz pilot engaged and destroyed the Syrian aircraft with both the AIM-9L Sidewinder and 20mm cannon.

25 May 1982
11 June 1982

F-16A, No. 240
Knights of the North Squadron, IASF

Amos Mohar
Yehuda Bavli

Netz No. 107 is seen preparing to touch down in this photograph taken in 2005. The aircraft is wearing the new tail art of the 'Flying Wing' Squadron. In 1990 the IASF became somewhat less restrictive regarding tail art and unit markings. Proudly displayed on the nose of 107 are the six and half kill markings obtained to date by this historic aircraft.

Netz 107 was a combat-tested veteran long before claiming six and half kills, having flown in one of the most daring combat missions of the IASF. On 7 June 1981 No. 107 flew in the first wave of F-16s that successfully took out Iraq's nuclear reactor during Operation OPERA. In the photograph 107 is also marked with the green triangular mission symbol underneath the cockpit to denote its participation in OPERA. (O. Zidon Collection)

In this particular photograph No. 240 is shown on the tarmac proudly displaying the three MiG kills acquired by Amos Mohar and Yehuda Bavli during 1982. The identity of the individual in the cockpit is unknown. However, it's doubtful if he's an Israeli pilot. (R. Weiss Collection)

F-16A-Block 10 78-0340 No. 240: aircraft destroyed: 2 MiG-21s; 1 Su-22: weapons: unknown; AIM-9L Sidewinder air-to-air missiles. On 25 May 1982 F-16A No. 240 was flown by Amos Mohar of the 'Knights of the North' when he was credited with downing two Syrian MiG-21s. Yehuda Bavli claimed a third Syrian MiG kill in F-16A No. 240 on 11 June 1982. No. 240 was lost on 10 April 1986.

8 June 1982
9 June 1982

F-16A, No. 250
Knights of the North Squadron, IASF

Avishai Canaan
Roi Tamir

In this photograph No. 250 appears on static display at an air show or open house at an unidentified air base in Israel. The F-16s of the 'Knights of the North' all had the tail art replaced with the newer design in the 1990s. (A. Dor Collection)

Adorned with the 'Red Dragons' Squadron's impressive new tail art, MiG killer No. 250 waits for clearance prior to take off. During 1982 Netz 250 was assigned to the 'Knights of the North' when it claimed two Syrian MiGs. Both Syrian jets were downed with AIM-9L Sidewinder heat-seeking air-to-air missiles. (O. Zidon Collection)

F-16A-Block 10B 78-0346 No. 250: aircraft destroyed: 1 MiG-23; 1 MiG-21: weapons: 2 AIM-9L Sidewinder missiles.

8 June 1982
11 June 1982
11 June 1982

F-16A, No. 225
Knights of the North Squadron, IASF

Shlomo Sas
Relik Shafir

F-16A-Block 5 78-0322 No. 129: aircraft destroyed: 1 MiG-23: weapon: AIM-9L Sidewinder air-to-air missile.

9 June 1982

F-16A, No. 243
Knights of the North Squadron, IASF

Avishai Canaan

F-16A-Block 10A 78-0342 No. 243: aircraft destroyed: 1 MiG-21: weapon: AIM 9L Sidewinder air-to-air missile.

The single-seat triple MiG killer No. 225 is captured in this image just prior to landing, gear down and airbrakes extended. No. 225 was lost during a training mission. (R. Weiss Collection)

F-16A-Block 10 78-0330 No. 225: aircraft destroyed: 1 MiG-23; 2 Su-22s: weapons: 2 Sidewinder AIM-9L air-to-air missiles; 1 AIM-9P3 Sidewinder air-to-air missile. This F-16A was lost on 7 December 1986 in a training accident due to engine failure. Captain Boaz Mehoria, No. 110 Squadron, was killed as a result.

9 June 1982

F-16A, No. 129
First Jet Squadron, IASF

Eytan Stibbe

Now assigned to the 'Flying Wing' Squadron F-16A No. 129 is seen blasting into the sky. The nose of the aircraft is marked with a shared kill roundel for a victory obtained on 9 June 1982 when Eytan Stibbe and Eliezer Shkedi of the 'First Jet' Squadron joined forces to down a Syrian MiG-23. (O. Zidon Collection)

Sparrowhawk No. 243 of the 'Golden Eagle' Squadron was captured in the above photograph as it streaks across the runway at Nevatim Air Base, home of the 'Golden Eagles'. This historic F-16A not only proved that the Sparrowhawk is an agile dogfighter, but is also quite capable of deep-penetration bombing missions.

Painted on the fuselage is the roundel for the MiG-21 kill accomplished on 9 June 1982 by Avishai Canaan. To the left of the Syrian MiG kill roundel is a green triangle which denotes that 243 was one of the eight F-16As that destroyed the nuclear reactor in Iraq on 7 June 1981, during Operation OPERA. (O. Zidon Collection)

F-16A No. 232 of the 'Golden Eagle' Squadron prepares to land after completing a training sortie. The Syrian roundel painted on the fuselage indicates that 232 has been credited with a single MiG kill during combat air operations on 9 June 1982. The 'Golden Eagle' Squadron operates both single- and two-seat Sparrowhawks. Many Sparrowhawks have entered into the upgrade programme but there are no external difference between the upgraded F-16s and the original aircraft. All the avionic changes and replacements are internal. (O. Zidon Collection)

Netz No. 220 from the 'Red Dragon' Squadron climbs into the clear skies over Ovda Air Base on full afterburner. This MiG killer is a member of the Israeli aggressor squadron, the 'Red Dragons', which practises enemy air tactics, and flies against all other IASF fighter squadrons. The Red Dragon Squadron training is very similar to the United States Air Force Red Flag exercises. (O. Zidon Collection)

9 June 1982

F-16A, No. 232
Knights of the North Squadron, IASF

Relik Shafir

F-16A-Block 10 78-0334 No. 232: aircraft destroyed: 1 MiG-21: weapon: AIM-9L Sidewinder air-to-air missile.

During the Lebanon War No. 223 was flying with the 'Knights of the North' when, on 9 June 1982, Relik Shafir downed a Syrian MiG-23 with an AIM-9L heat-seeking missile. The IASF name for the AIM-9L is Loolav. (Palm Branch)

F-16A/B 223, now deployed with the 'Red Dragons' Squadron, is captured by the camera in a high speed take-off from Ovda Air Base, home of the IASF aggressor squadron. The 'Red Dragons' Squadron was formed in 2005 for the enhancement of IASF pilots in combat scenarios. During May 2006 the 'Red Dragons' Squadron acted as the Red Force in a joint exercise with the United States Air Force. This overpowering photograph of No.223 depicts the raw power of the F-16A/B Netz. (O. Zidon Collection)

A pair of 'Golden Eagle' Squadron F-16s, No. 998 and MiG killer No. 255 are preparing for takeoff. On 9 June 1982 No. 255 was assigned to the 'Knights of the North' when Avi Lavi engaged an enemy aircraft and, during the ensuing air battle, was able to obtain position on a Syrian MiG-21. Upon obtaining a good missile tone he launched a heat-seeking Sidewinder missile which flew true to the target, destroying the MiG. (O. Zidon Collection)

9 June 1982

F-16A, No. 220
Knights of the North Squadron, IASF

Amir Nachumi

F-16A-Block 10 78-0327 No. 220: aircraft destroyed: 1 MiG-21: weapon: AIM-9L Sidewinder air-to-air missile.

9 June 1982

F-16A, No. 223
Knights of the North Squadron, IASF

Relik Shafir

F-16A Block 10 78-0329 No. 223: Aircraft destroyed: 1 MiG-21: weapon: AIM-9L Sidewinder air-to-air missile.

9 June 1982

F-16A, No. 255
Knights of the North Squadron, IASF

Avi Lavi

F-16A-Block 10B 78-0255 No. 255: aircraft destroyed: 1 MiG-21: weapon: AIM-9L Sidewinder air-to-air missile.

9 June 1982

F-16A, No. 290
Ha Negve Squadron, IASF

Pilot Unknown

F-16A-Block 10D 80-0664 No. 290: aircraft destroyed: 2 MiG-23s: weapons: AIM-9L Sidewinder air-to-air missiles.

F-16 No. 290 is another double MiG killer from the 1982 war in Lebanon. In this undated photograph 290 displays two Syrian roundels denoting the aircraft's victories. On 17 January 1995 Netz 290 collided with F-16 No. 269 near Palmachim, Israel. The pilot, Captain Danny Oberst, who was flying 269 didn't survive the collision. However, the pilot of 290, identified only as Y, did survive. Both aircraft were assigned to No. 110 Squadron at the time of the collision. (A. Dor Collection)

On 10 June 1982, in the skies over Lebanon, Israeli F-16A Netzes claimed thirteen aerial combat victories over Syrian MiGs. Among the victories claimed that day was the one credited to No. 138, flown by Ami Lustig of the 'First Jet' Squadron. The Lustig kill was one of only five made during the second Lebanon War with the F-16's 20mm cannon. Now assigned to the 'Flying Wing' Squadron this historic jet is seen climbing into a blue Israeli sky in a high speed full afterburner take-off. (O. Zidon Collection)

10 June 1982

F-16A, No. 138
First Jet Squadron, IASF

Ami Lustig

F-16A-Block 5 78-0325 No. 138: aircraft destroyed: 1 MiG-23: weapon: cannon.

10 June 1982
F-16A, No. 237
Knights of the North Squadron, IASF

Amir Nahumi

Opher Einav

F-16A-Block 10A 78-0338 No. 237: aircraft destroyed: 2 MiG-23s; 1 MiG-21: weapons: AIM-9L Sidewinder AAMs. During the

Appearing in this somewhat grainy photograph No. 237 was captured taxiing on the taxi-way of an unidentified air base. The wingtips of the F-16 as a rule are armed with live air-to-air missiles when not involved in training missions. No. 237 was lost as the direct result of an engine stall over the Negev Desert on 2 February 2000. When the pilot attempted to relight the stalled engine it caught fire, forcing him to eject. (A. Dor Collection)

The first photograph of No. 234 depicts the aircraft taxiing to the main runway prior to taking off for a training sortie. The 'Red Dragons' Squadron operates from Ovda Air Force Base, where it specializes in flying enemy tactics not only for Israeli aircrews, but also for other friendly nations. (O. Zidon Collection)

The second photograph shows No. 234 with its unique dragon-tail artwork launching from Ovda AB. As well as the identifying tail art 234 has been marked with three Syrian MiG kills. All three victories are credited to Amir Nachumi of the 'Knights of the North' Squadron. (O. Zidon Collection)

10 June 1982

F-16A, No. 234
Knights of the North Squadron, IASF

Amir Nachumi

F-16A-Block 10A 78-0336 No. 234: aircraft destroyed: 3 MiG-23s: weapons: 1 manoeuvre; 2 AIM-9 Sidewinder air-to-air missiles.

Netz No. 111 of the 'Flying Wing' Squadron is adorned with two kill markings from the Lebanon War as well as the green triangle which identifies 111 as one of the strike aircraft that participated in the attack on the Iraqi nuclear reactor in 1981. No. 111 demonstrates a full-power take-off using its afterburner. The photograph was taken as the 'Flying Wing' MiG killer departed Ovda Air Base. (O. Zidon Collection)

Lebanon War the Syrian Arab Air Force attempted to challenge the IASF's control of the skies over Lebanon and paid dearly for its efforts. On 10 June alone IASF F-15s and F-16s destroyed eighteen Syrian MiGs. Amir Nahumi, flying with the 'Knights of the North', claimed three victories, downing two MiG-23s and a MiG-21 during one mission. The three kills, added to Nahumi's tally, gave him five kills as of 10 June 1982. He would go on to claim two more Syrian MiGs on 11 June 1982 to give him a total of seven kills in the Netz.

10 June 1982

F-16A, No. 111
Yahalom/Diamond
First Jet Squadron, IASF

Sasha Levin

FF-16A-Block 5 78-0313 No. 111: aircraft destroyed: 1 MiG-21; 1 Gazelle: weapon: 2 AIM-9L Sidewinder air-to-air missiles.

10 June 1982

F-16A, No. 116
First Jet Squadron, IASF

Rafi Berkovich

F-16A-Block 5 78-0137 No. 116: aircraft destroyed: 2 MiG-23s; 1 MiG-21: weapons: 2 AIM-9L Sidewinder air-to-air missiles; 1 cannon.

This triple MiG killer from the Lebanon War in 1982 was photographed utilizing brute force in its take-off from Ovda Air Base. No. 116 is showing off the sleek lines of the F-16 clearly in the bright blue sky. Little information is available regarding the aerial victories of this Netz. (O. Zidon Collection)

Close up photo of F-16A No. 118 as it taxis to take off. Painted on the nose of the F-16 Netz is a Syrian roundel denoting 118's victory over a MiG-23 during air operations on 10 June 1982. F-16A 118 is yet another of the historic F-16s involved in Operation OPERA on 7 June 1981. No. 118 flew in Eshkol flight, call sign Eshkol 03. (O. Zidon Collection)

10 June 1982

F-16A, No. 118
First Jet Squadron, IASF

Hagai Katz

F-16A- Block 16A 78-0318 No. 118: aircraft destroyed: 1 MiG-23: weapon: AIM-9L Sidewinder air-to-air missile.

MiG killer Netz No. 124 is marked with a single roundel denoting a MiG-23 kill on 10 June 1982. There is little information available regarding the aerial victory noted on the nose of the aircraft. Sometime after this photograph was taken the 'Negev' Squadron, like other Netz squadrons, introduced the new tail art to their aircraft. No. 124, however, is adorned with the new tail art of the 'Red Dragons' Squadron. (A. Dor Collection)

10 June 1982

F-16A, No. 124
Kochav/Star
First Jet Squadron, IASF

Shlomo Zaytman

F-16A-Block 5 78-0320 No. 124: aircraft destroyed: 1 MiG-23: weapon: 1 AIM-9L Sidewinder air-to-air missile.

11 June 1982

F-16A, No. 254
First Jet Squadron, IASF

Dani Oshrat

F-16A-Block 10B 78-0348 No. 254: aircraft destroyed: 1 MiG-21; 1 Su-22: Weapon: 2 AIM-9L Sidewinder air-to-air missiles.

11 June 1982

F-16A, No. 258
First Jet Squadron, IASF

Major Rani Falk

F-16A-Block 10C 78-0351 No. 258: aircraft destroyed: 1 Su-22; 1 MiG-21: weapon: M61 Vulcan 20mm cannon. Throughout the Lebanon War the F-16 Netz not only proved to be the primary

Sometime after 1982 the double MiG killer was re-assigned to the 'Golden Eagle' Squadron. These photographs depict the jet in two different flight configurations. In the first shot 254 is flying off the wing of another F-16 over the Israeli desert, while the second depicts the MiG killer just prior to landing. (A. Hershko / O. Zidon Collection)

strike aircraft for the IASF, but also a capable MiG killer. On 11 June 1982, the last day of the war, F-16s of the IASF claimed thirteen Syrian aircraft while engaged in air-to-ground operations. During air operations one of the 'First Jet' Squadron pilots, Major Rafi, engaged three Syrian MiGs. With the F-16's internal M61A1 20mm cannon he shot down an Su-22 and a MiG-21. Rafi is also credited with the first ever aerial victory in the F-16.

Netz No. 258 is pictured in the first shot just moments before touching down at Nevatim Air Base, having been re-assigned from Ramon Air Base in 2003. In this particular photograph 258 is painted in the standard Netz colour scheme and wearing the tail markings of the 'Golden Eagle' Squadron. (O. Zidon Collection)

In the second photograph No. 258 is taxiing to a parking spot on the tarmac after completing a training mission. (O. Zidon Collection)

11 June 1982

F-16A, No. 252
First Jet Squadron, IASF

Amos Bar

F-16A-Block 10B 78-0347 No. 252: aircraft destroyed: 1 Su-22: weapon: cannon.

On 11 June 1982 Amos Bar was flying F-16A No. 252 when he was credited with the downing of a Syrian Su-22 with 20mm cannon-fire. The aerial victory of 11 June was not Bar's first kill. In fact this was number eight for the former Shahak pilot. His seven prior kills were while he was assigned to No. 117 Squadron. The 'Golden Eagle' Squadron now claims ownership of No. 252 where the aircraft continues to fly combat operations. (O. Zidon Collection)

11 June 1982

F-16A, No. 246
Knights of the North Squadron, IASF

Roi Tamir

F-16A-Block-10B 78-0346 No. 246: aircraft destroyed: 1 MiG-21: weapon: AIM-9L Sidewinder air-to-air missile.

June 1982

F-16A, No. 272
Ha Negve Squadron, IASF

Moshe Rozenfeld

F-16A-Block 10C 78-0653 No. 272: aircraft destroyed: 1 MiG-21; ½ MiG-23: weapons: unknown.

During Operation PEACE FOR GALILEE on 11 June 1982 Roi Tamir claimed a second aerial victory flying F-16A No. 246. Now with the 'Golden Eagle' Squadron the MiG killer is about to touch down after completing a training sortie. (O. Zidon Collection)

In this image F-16A No. 272 is captured in detail in a full afterburner take-off. Markings on the nose of the fuselage indicate that this aircraft has been credited with 1.5 aerial combat victories. Little information is available regarding these victories at the time of writing. (O. Zidon Collection)

7 August 2006

F-16C, No. 364
Knights of the North Squadron, IASF

Classified

F-16C-Block 30 No. 364: aircraft destroyed: 1 Ababil unmanned aerial vehicle: weapon: Python-4 air-to-air missile.

13 August 2006

F-16D, No. 074
Valley Squadron, IASF

Classified

F-16D-Block 30 No. 074: aircraft destroyed: 1 Ababil unmanned aerial vehicle: weapon: Python 5 air-to-air missile.

'Knights of the North' Squadron Barak 1 is seen standing on the tarmac displaying a unique kill marking. The uniqueness of the kill marking on the nose of Nos. 364 and F-16D 074 is in its design. The roundel depicts the national colours and emblem (cedar tree) of Lebanon, ignoring Hezbollah. The single-seat fighter was credited on 7 August 2006 with shooting down a Hezbollah Ababil unmanned vehicle (UAV) with a single Rafael Python all aspect air-to-air missile. (O. Zidon Collection)

F-16D Block 30 Barak 1 from the 'Valley' Squadron appears in the sand camouflage of light green and brown on top and grey on the underside of the aircraft. Like F-16C No. 364 it was credited with downing a Hezbollah Ababil UAV during August 2006. However, the 13 August 2006 kill was accomplished with the Rafael Python 5, the newest of the Python air-to-air missiles in the IASF inventory. (O. Zidon Collection)

6 October 2012

F-16I, No. 844
One Squadron, IASF

Classified

F-16I-Block 30 No. 844: aircraft destroyed: unknown type unmanned aerial vehicle: weapon: Python-5 air-to-air missile.

On 6 October 2012 Israeli radar units began tracking an unidentified unmanned drone operating over the Mediterranean Sea. The drone was tracked by radar when it was established that it had crossed into Israeli airspace. The IASF scrambled F-16Is from the 'One' Squadron based at Ramon Air Base to intercept the drone. When the drone was intercepted by the 'One' Squadron jets, it was quickly determined that it was unarmed and appeared to be on a surveillance mission. The crew of F-16I No. 844 was ordered to destroy the drone which was engaged over the Negev desert and destroyed by an Israeli Python-5 AAM.

The 'One' Squadron Sufa No. 844 credited with bringing down the drone is captured in this photograph in graceful climb on a training sortie. It has been determined that the drone downed by F-16I No. 844 was an Iranian made UAV despatched by Hezbollah on a surveillance mission into Israel.

25 April 2013

F-16C, No. 340
First Jet Squadron, IASF

Classified

F-16C-Block 40 No. 340; aircraft destroyed: unknown type unmanned aerial vehicle (UAV); Weapon: air-to-air missile.

On 25 April 2013 for the second time in a seven-week period the Israeli air defence system detected an unidentified aircraft attempting to enter Israeli air space from Lebanon. All indications suggest that the UAV took off from the area between Tyre and Sidon.

IASF F-16 Baraks of the First Jet Squadron were scrambled to intercept the intruder. The UAV was acquired, deemed to be a hostile aircraft and attacked and shot down by an Israeli pilot flying Barak No. 340.

Chapter Nine

Operation OPERA – 7 June 1981

The following text (both quoted and paraphrased) regarding the 7 June 1981 Zroa Ha'Avir Ve'Halalal air strike on the Iraqi nuclear power plant is provided with the permission of Tsahi Ben-Ami from an article he published in *Combat Aircraft Magazine*, Vol. 6, No. 2, 2006.

The Israel DF/AF has been involved in a lot of active service over the years, but few of its operations remain more notable than Operation OPERA, a daring raid against an Iraqi nuclear reactor being used by Saddam Hussein's regime to develop a significant nuclear strike capability. Much of the story has remained under a cloak of secrecy ever since.

Between 1972 and 1976 Iraq's nuclear weapons programme got underway in earnest. Its initial goal was to acquire a complete safeguarded fuel cycle able to produce separated plutonium. For this purpose, Iraq secretly signed an agreement with the French government to supply a 40MWth MTR reactor called Tammuz-1 or Osiris.

Mossad, the Israeli intelligence service, along with experts from Israeli Defence Force Intelligence, had determined that the French reactor and Italian laboratories would be in a position to supply Hussein's Ba'ath party with as many as four nuclear weapons per year.

With the intelligence gathered by Mossad about the potential nuclear capabilities of Iraq, along with the mindset of Saddam Hussein, who proclaimed in a speech on 29 October 1979 that 'The law of Muhammad lies in the sword, while the law of Saddam lies in the Atom', the evidence was clear that the Tammuz 1 project (Tammuz was the Babylonian God of Hell) was a direct threat to the State of Israel. The question of what would Israel do had been resolved. Destroy the reactor! The only question left was: could it be done?

Knowing that it would not be an easy task, the IASF was ordered to conduct feasibility studies to establish if an air strike could be accomplished. After months of evaluation, which took into account everything from risk to the strike force, aircraft selection, pilot selection, and countless hours of training in which the pilots had absolutely no idea what kind of mission they were training for, 'In February 1980 came the results of these trials'. Major General David Ivry told Defence Minister Ezer Weizman, 'it could be done.'

In the original operational plan the IASF had selected the F-4E Kurnass as the principal aircraft to destroy the reactor. However, in 1979 US Secretary of Defense, Harold Brown, was on a trip to the Middle East when he offered seventy-five F-16A/B Falcons to the Israeli government . The offer was quickly accepted by the IASF.

On 2 July 1980 the first F-16s arrived at Ramat David Air Base where they were assigned to the 'First Jet' Squadron. The IASF squadrons began training for the mission, concentrating on attacking infrastructural targets and testing the capability of the F-16 to reach the planned range. Simulated bombing missions with different weapons-system configurations were also conducted and evaluated. The end result was that the F-16 would fly one of the most adventurous and daring missions the IASF had ever undertaken.

Like the aircraft chosen for the OPERA mission, the pilots would have to be the Zroa Ha'Avir Ve'Halalal elite. The eight strike pilots chosen were truly an extraordinary group of combat-tested pilots with exceptional flying skills and undaunted courage. The two F-16 flights flew under the call signs Eshkol and Izmal with Eshkol the first on target.

The pilots of Eshkol flight have been publicly identified as: Ze'ev Raz (Eshkol Leader), Amos Yadlin (Eshkol 02), Dubi Yaffe (Eshkol 03) and Hagai Katz (Eshkol 04). Amir Nahumi was Izmal Leader, with Yiftach Spector (Izmal 02), Relik Shafir (Izmal 03) and Ilan Ramon (Izmal 04). (Ilan Ramon would go on to be the first Israeli astronaut, later killed in the space shuttle Columbia disaster).

On Time, On Target

Time to launch. The government of Israel had authorized the attack, aircraft and pilots were selected, training missions completed and intelligence had been evaluated, establishing that the threat level to IASF pilots would be high. Since the Iran/Iraq war the defences around the reactor had been improved significantly. The strike force would face an array of Russian ground-to-air SA-2, SA-3, SA-4 and SA-7 Strela missiles, and the ever-present Iraqi Air Force with their Russian MiGs. The Iraqis had also built a high and wide wall around the reactor to help protect the reactor containment building.

On 7 June 1982 the eight strike aircraft of Eshkol and Izmal flights with their escorting F-15 Bazs departed the relative safety of the skies of Israel for the Al-Tuwaitha site seventeen kilometres (almost ten and a half miles) south of Baghdad. The F-15s were tasked with dealing with any air threat that could endanger the strike aircraft. These F-15s would be configured with a variety of air-to-air weaponry in order to accomplish their mission. The combat air patrol aircraft would surely have been accompanied by a modified F-15B serving as a flying command post during the mission. The crew of this aircraft would have the authority for the 'go/no go' order for the mission.

General Amos Yadlin (Eshkol 02) takes up the story: 'We flew through the south of Jordan and headed into the Arabian Desert.' Continuing on its way, the strike force passed through Saudi Arabian air space into Iraq. The flight flew on till hitting the fourth waypoint, a large lake located fifty kilometres (about thirty-one miles) west of Baghdad. It wasn't long before the IASF aircraft descended to a hundred feet upon entering Iraqi air space, to prevent the strike aircraft from exposure for the first time to Iraqi radar and placing the Israelis within a surface-to-air missile kill zone. At a predetermined point Eshkol and Izmal flights would pop up to 7,000 feet for an accurate aim at the target with a 35-degree angle of attack.

General Yadlin: 'We crossed the shore, on the right, a bus full of tourists; colourful taxis and people having fun. Just four miles before the pull-up point. I turn on the radar and see no MiGs. Ten miles to go and Raz (Eshkol Leader) breaks radio silence: "pay attention to ground fire!"'

Then the chaos begins.

Flashes fill the sky, followed by little puffs of smoke. I push the throttle forward and engage full afterburner. I pull up and see the wall and then bright in the dusk light I see the reactor's silver dome. I'm at 6,500 feet and pulling 7Gs rolling over, flying inverted, gaining speed. The pipper slowly follows the trajectory line. I released the bombs; break hard and to the left, look for missiles in the air. One zooms below me and impacts with the ground. I climb in full power to rejoin the flight.

After the raid, Raz asked the pilots to call in, but there was no reply from Izmal 04. This was Ilan Ramon, the last pilot to attack the reactor and thereby exposed to the greatest risk. Raz made another attempt. 'Izmal 04, are you OK?'

'OK, OK I pulled out of it – I'm OK! Izmal 04 Charlie!' Charlie was the code for full success. Target destroyed two bombs overshot.

On the way out the strike force flew as high as they could and were only challenged by one Iraqi MiG that closed but did not engage.

Eshkol and Izmal flights had destroyed the Tammuz-1 nuclear reactor, the 'jewel in the crown' of Saddam Hussein's nuclear programme.

The F-16 Netz (Sparrowhawk) of Operation OPERA

7 June 1981

F-16A, No. 113
First Jet Squadron, IASF

Lieutenant Colonel Ze'ev Raz
(Eshkol 01)

On 7 June 1981 Lieutenant Colonel Raz piloted this jet during the OPERA raid and was the first attack aircraft to hit the reactor. During the raid No. 113 was configured with two 2,000lb Mk-84 bombs. (O. Zidon Collection)

The tail art on No. 113 in the second inflight photograph indicates that this F-16 has been re-assigned to the 'Golden Eagle' Squadron. On the nose of the aircraft is the green triangle which identifies it as one of the attacking aircraft during the historic OPERA raid. (O. Zidon Collection)

F-16A-Block 16A 78-0315 No. 113: F-16A No. 113 is seen taxiing under a cloudy overcast sky, configured for an air-to-air mission with four Sidewinder missiles.

7 June 1981

F-16A, No. 107
First Jet Squadron, IASF

Amos Yadlin
(Eshkol 02)

In this inflight photograph Netz 107 appears in the new tail markings of the 'Flying Wing' Squadron. During 1982 this historic F-16A was assigned to the 'First Jet' Squadron when the 6.5 aerial combat victories were obtained by three different pilots, Zeev Raz (one), Eliezer Shkedi (two) and Eytan Stibbe (four). (O. Zidon Collection)

F-16A-Block 5 78-0311 No. 107: Sparrowhawk 107 is presently the leading IASF MiG killer with 6.5 kills. On 7 June 1981 No. 107 was flown by Amos Yadlin during the raid on the Iraqi nuclear reactor near Baghdad. Yadlin was flying on the wing of Lieutenant Colonel Raz and followed him down the chute. Both pilots successfully placed their 2,000lb bombs on target. The bombs were equipped with delayed fuses and penetrators thus ensuring explosion deep in the reactor core to maximize the damage.

7 June 1981

F-16A, No. 118
First Jet Squadron, IASF

Dobbi Yaffe
(Eshkol 03)

F-16A-Block 16A 78-0318 No. 118: The F-16s from the 'First Jet' and the 'Knights of the North' Squadrons faced a formidable task during the raid on Saddam's nuclear reactor. The reactor site was protected by its own air defence system with anti-aircraft guns and surface-to-air missiles. 'First Jet' squadron F-16A No. 118 flew in Eshkol flight.

An unidentified IASF pilot is captured in this photograph taxiing 118 after a long-range mission. Netz 118 is equipped with the standard centreline fuel tank and two additional 370-gallon external fuel tanks.

In the photograph 118 is seen in the tail markings of the 'Golden Wing' Squadron and still proudly wearing a single kill marking from the Lebanon War along with the Operation OPERA marking in recognition of its participation in the raid of 7 June 1981. The second picture is a close up of No. 118 with its distinguished war record displayed on the fuselage. (O. Zidon Collection)

Power and grace are accented in this Ofer Zidon photograph of No. 129 as the jet climbs into a clear Middle Eastern sky. The new tail art on Netz 129 indicates that the jet is now assigned to the 'Flying Wing' Squadron. The half roundel on the nose indicates that No. 129 has been credited with a shared kill obtained during the Lebanon War. (O. Zidon Collection)

7 June 1981

F-16A, No. 129
First Jet Squadron, IASF

Hagai Katz
(Eshkol 04)

F-16A-Block 16A - 78-0322 No. 129: No. 129 was the last IASF F-16 in Eshkol flight to hit the Iraqi nuclear reactor. The eight attacking F-16s hit the nuclear complex at five-second intervals. A total of

sixteen 2,000lb Mk-84 bombs were dropped on the complex with fourteen direct hits. IASF mission planners figured that it would take eight bombs to destroy the reactor.

7 June 1981

F-16A, No. 228
Knights of the North Squadron, IASF

Lieutenant Colonel Amir Nachumi
(Izmal 01)

No. 228 is seen in the standard camouflage of the F-16 Netz. This aircraft belongs to the 'Golden Wing' Squadron which now operates both single- and two-seat Netzes. No. 228 was one of the IASF F-16s to take part in Operation ARATZA 19 (DRUGSTORE) which destroyed the Syrian missile sites in the Beqaa Valley during the Lebanon War. (O. Zidon Collection)

No. 249 captured in a full afterburner take off on a training sortie. During the raid 249 was flown by triple ace Yiftach Spector who flew in Izmal flight as Izmal 02. (O. Zidon Collection)

F-16A-Block 10 78-0332 No. 228: F-16A No. 228 was the lead aircraft in the second strike flight during the raid on the reactor. This aircraft was flown during the 1,000-mile round trip by Lieutenant Colonel Amir Nachumi, the squadron leader of the 'Knights of the North' Squadron. Nachumi was the first IASF pilot to claim a fixed-wing aerial victory in the F-16 when he downed a Syrian MiG. He is also credited with over 300 combat missions, and is one of only a few pilots in the Zroa Ha'Avir Ve'Halalal who is an acknowledged ace in two different aircraft types.

7 June 1981

F-16A, No. 249
Knights of the North Squadron, IASF

Yiftach Spector
(Izmal 02)

F-16A-Block 10A 78-0345 No. 249: Izmal 02 was flown by retired General Yiftach Spector, a triple ace, with fifteen confirmed aerial victories. It goes without saying that, with the inclusion of pilots like Yiftach Spector in the OPERA mission, the State of Israel used the elite pilots of the IASF.

7 June 1981

F-16A, No. 239
Knights of the North Squadron, IASF

Relik Shafir
(Izmal 03)

General Spector is captured by the camera standing alongside an F-16. The General obtained ace status in three different aircraft, Shahak, Nesher and Kurnass. (O. Zidon / P. Mersky Collections)

Netz No. 239 with engine in full afterburner blasts into the skies over its home base. If you've never witnessed it, the full afterburner take-off is an impressive show of sight and sound. (O. Zidon Collection)

F-16A-Block 10A 78-0339 No. 239: The eight F-16s of Eshkol and Izmal flights flew just one hundred feet off the ground in the 600 miles to Baghdad to avoid radar detection. The planning and skill of the IASF pilots was rewarded when it became obvious that they had completely surprised the Iraqi defences protecting the reactor.

Often overlooked in Operation OPERA were the IASF units supporting the mission. Other assets included a Grummam E-2C Hawkeye, a Boeing 707 jamming/command aircraft, a 707 tanker and two sections of F-15s, all of which were available if the strike force ran into problems.

7 June 1981

F-16A, No. 243
Knights of the North Squadron, IASF

Ilan Ramon
(Izmal 04)

F-16A-Block 10A 78-0342 No. 243: The last Netz down the chute on 7 June 1981 was No. 243 flown by Ilan Ramon. This position is without a doubt the least desirable of all the flight positions during a bombing run. By the time the last flight member is on his bomb run every enemy gunner knows he's coming. Even though Ramon faced the most intensive anti-aircraft fire he was able to avoid being shot down and placed his two 2,000lb bombs on target.

Of all the IASF pilots involved Ilan Ramon was the least experienced but, in the true tradition of the IASF, he accomplished his mission. This outstanding pilot would go on to become the first Israeli astronaut, only to be killed in the space shuttle Columbia disaster.

No. 243 from Nevatim Air Base is on static display at an air show in Bino-Turnay, Czech Republic. The photograph was taken on 4 September 2004 by Miloslav Vasicek who has kindly allowed its use in this book. This is the F-16 flown by Colonel Ramon during the attack on the Osirak nuclear plant. (M. Vasicek Collection)

Postscript Operation OPERA

The attack on the Osirak nuclear facility was widely critized by most of the world, which also rejected the Israeli claim that the air strike was done in self defence. 'Information gathered after the First Gulf War made clear the situation regarding Iraq's weapons capabilities.' New evidence proved that the raid was justified and necessary. If the Israelis had not destroyed the reactor when they did the Iraqi invasion of Kuwait in 2000 would have looked a lot different than it did. If Saddam Hussein's military had possessed nuclear weapons neither Gulf War would have taken place. The consequences of waiting until Iraq had obtained nuclear weapons would have been horrendous. It's in no way too farfetched to believe that the unstable Hussein government would have used nuclear weapons in its quest to control the Middle East.

The IASF raid was a success in that it put the complex out of commission and set back Saddam's nuclear weapons' programme. The Osirak facility remained heavily damaged and un-repaired. During the First Gulf War United States air strikes finally destroyed the site completely.

The IASF raid on the nuclear site was considered a success. However, many don't know how close it came to being a complete disaster. On 7 June 1981 King Hussein of Jordan was holidaying on his yacht in Aqaba when he saw the strike aircraft on their way to Iraq. The King contacted the Saudis to alert them. The Saudi military was unable to make radar contact with the IASF jets and dismissed the report.

What was the response of Saddam Hussein's regime to the raid? As a result of Operation OPERA the Commander of the Western Air Defence Zone, Iraqi Air Force Colonel Fakhri Hussein Jafer, and all officers in his command over the rank of major, were executed. Twenty-three other Iraqi Air Force officers and pilots were sent to prison.

Israel was publicly condemned by countries all over the world, including the United States, and the United Nations. However, privately, even countries in the Middle East were pleased. One American, Secretary of Defense Dick Cheney, in 1991 sent to Major General David Ivry, a satellite reconnaissance photograph of the destroyed power plant to express his appreciation for Operation OPERA. The photograph was inscribed: 'thanks for an outstanding job … it made our job easier in DESERT STORM. Dick Cheney.'

Chapter Ten
Operation ORCHARD 6 September 2007

On 6 September 2007, in the dead of night, eight strike aircraft took off from an air base in Israel on a highly classified mission into northern Syria near the Turkish border. The IASF F-15I Ra'ams and F-16I Sufas were armed with AGM-65 Maverick air-to-ground missiles, laser-guided bombs, and electronic jamming equipment.

Operation ORCHARD was designed by the Zroa Ha'Avir Ve'Halalal to be a surgical air strike against a joint Syrian and North Korean nuclear facility in the Syrian Desert. Unconfirmed reports suggest that four of the attacking aircraft crossed into Syrian airspace undetected by radar. It's worth pointing out that

At this point it's a fairly safe bet that it was elements of the Zroa Ha'Avir Ve'Halalal that destroyed the Syrian reactor on 6 September 2007. The attack would have been carried out by F-15I Ra'am of the 'Hammer' Squadron based at Hatzerim Air Force Base. It's not certain if Ra'am (Thunder) 238 was an actual participant in the raid. In this photograph the powerful jet sits in a hardened shelter armed with two Have Nap (Popeye) cruise missiles. (O. Zidon Collection)

It's rumoured that F-16I Sufas were also part of the original strike force during the first wave of attacking IASF fighters. In this photograph two F-16Is are positioned at the end of the runway awaiting orders to launch. Again it's not certain if these two aircraft from the 'One' Squadron took part in the raid. However, the F-16Is that did participate would have been armed in the same manner as the heavily-loaded F-16Is in this photograph. (O. Zidon Collection)

Syria and a number of Arab countries are all equipped with the Russian-made Pantsyr-2A/TOR-M1 air defence system. The Pantsyr/TOR-M1 radar, surface-to-air missiles (eight surface-to-air missiles on each launcher) and 30mm Gatling-gun system have been deployed with the Russian claim that it is immune to

Any Israeli aircraft involved in a deep penetration combat mission outside Israel would be protected by the Israeli F-15 Bazs. It is standard operational procedure that these high value assets (F-15/F-16Is) are provided with a combat air patrol during any such mission. The pilots tasked to fly the CAP mission would certainly all be handpicked pilots. (O. Zidon Collection)

electronic jamming. At the time of the attack on Syria's Al Kibar nuclear reactor it is reported that the Syrians had twenty-nine of the systems on line. How then did the IASF fly into the night sky out over the Mediterranean across the Euphrates river and successfully attack with laser-guided weapons the secret nuclear reactor at Al Kibar?

The Israelis have never publicly acknowledged that it was their aircraft that destroyed the Syrian/North Korean nuclear reactor under construction at Al Kibar. The Syrians have only acknowledged that the Israelis did enter Syrian airspace, dropped a few bombs, hit nothing and were driven off.

I would suggest that the evidence indicates that it was the IASF that carried out the attack at Al Kibar. One can speculate regarding the details surrounding the air strike that destroyed the reactor but, as always with the Israelis, details on any of their military operations just aren't forthcoming.

One theory that is widely accepted is that the Zroa Ha'Avir Ve'Halalal had included in the strike force one or more Gulfstream G550 aircraft, equipped with the IAI Elta EL/2085 (ELINT) intelligence-gathering system, and electronic warfare aircraft. Coupled with the F-15Is' electronic warfare capabilities they just simply and with brute force electronically attacked and shut down the air defence of the Syrians. It is further speculated that, after rendering the air defences useless, the attacking aircraft took a critical radar station out with laser-guided weapons. It was then just a quick eighteen-mile flight to Al Kibar where the IASF executed a surgical strike somewhat reminiscent of the destruction in Iraq of the Osirak reactor.

Chapter Eleven

Special Mission Aircraft of the Zroa Ha'Avir Ve'Halalal

In his book *Fly with the Israeli Air Force* Ofer Zidon writes:

Special Missions is the politically correct title of a host of such activities as: ELINT (Electronic Intelligence), (covering both COMINT (Communications Intelligence) and SIGINT (Signals Intelligence), EW (Electronic Warfare), communications relay and IMINT (Imagery Intelligence). The IDF/AF has always emphasized Special Missions, but from the mid-1970s investments, resources and efforts put into Special Missions increased considerably in light of the principal Yom Kippur War lessons: Intelligence, Communications and Precision.

From 1978 until 1994 the Israelis operated a fleet of four Grumman E-2C Hawkeye Airborne Early Warning (AEW) aircraft designed to give not only real-time air-to-air intelligence, but also provide real-time battlefield intelligence to Israeli ground forces. In November 1979 the E-2Cs were joined by the Israeli Aircraft Industries (IAI) Zahavan UAV which revolutionized the field of real-time Imagery Intelligence (IMINT) for the Israelis.

With the ever-changing environment in the field of electronic warfare the older Grumman E-2C Hawkeyes and the first generation Zahavan UAV have been phased-out of the Zroa Ha'Avir Ve'Halalal inventory. Both systems have been replaced with the most sophisticated aircraft and electronic technology available.

The E-2C Hawkeye, known as the Daya (Kite) by the Israelis, has been replaced by a fleet of Gulfstream GV Nachshon aircraft. On 26 June 2005 the first Nachshon signal intelligence (SIGINT) aircraft arrived at Lod Air Base. All the onboard electronic equipment for the Nachshon aircraft has been designed and built by the Israeli Aerospace Industry, Elta Group (IAI).

The Gulfstream GV Nachshon Special Electronic Mission Aircraft (SEMA) has been picked to replace the ageing Boeing 707 Re'en Signal Intelligence (SIGINT) aircraft. The G500/G550s have been equipped with all-Israeli Aerospace Industry, Elta Group, designed and built onboard electronic equipment. The Nachshon depicted in this photograph is No. 637 which was flown to Lod Air Base sometime during February 2006. (O. Zidon Collection)

There are presently two versions of IASF Nachshon G500/550 special mission aircraft. The GV Shavit SIGINT Nachshon is equipped with the IAI EL/I-3001 Airborne Integrated SIGINT (AISIS) Intelligence System. The second version is the G550 Aitam Conformal Airborne Early Warning Aircraft (CAEW). The G550 is outfitted with the IAI Elta EL/W-2085 system which enables the aircraft to support a variety missions such as:

- Long Range Air Surveillance
- Airborne C41 for Air and Naval Operations
- Airborne Command and Control Post
- Network Centric Warfare Operations
- Communication Node

Specification for Gulfstream GV 500/550

Crew: Classified
Aircraft Type: Fixed Wing, twin-engine
Power Plant: Two Turbofan BMW/Rolls Royce BR 700–710C411
Length: 96 feet 5 inches
Wingspan: 93 feet 4 inches
Height: 25 feet 11 inches
Maximum Speed: 672mph
Maximum Take-off Weight: 90,500 pounds
Range: 6,300 miles
Service Ceiling: 51,000 feet

IASF Unmanned Aerial Vehicle Fleet

The art of aerial intelligence gathering can be traced back for hundreds of years. In America the use of aerial reconnaissance was first documented during the Civil War when both Northern and Southern troops used hot-air balloons to observe enemy troop movements, artillery positions, and how troops were being positioned on the battlefield prior to engagement.

The field of intelligence collection in all its forms continues to evolve. One of the most prolific examples of the successful deployment of unmanned aerial vehicles (UAVs) in an operational combat environment without a doubt would be Operation MOLE CRICKET 19.

Operation MOLE CRICKET 19 was launched on 9 June 1982 by the Zroa Ha'Avir Ve'Halalal during the onset of the 1982 Lebanon War. MOLE CRICKET 19 was designed to seek out and destroy Syrian surface-to-air missile and anti-aircraft sites in the Beqaa Valley.

The ability and capabilities of the Israelis was completely underestimated by the Syrians and mother Russia, the major supplier of Syrian military equipment. The Syrians had ringed the Beqaa Valley with approximately twenty-eight surface-to-air missile sites (SA-2s, SA-3s and SA-6s) and their controlling radars. Israeli remotely piloted vehicles (RPVs) discovered the deployment of an additional five SA-6 missiles from the Golan Heights into the Beqaa Valley.

With the discovery of the deployment of the SA-6s from the Golan Heights, Operation MOLE CRICKET 19 was set in motion. Once the command was given, the Israelis launched a number of ADM-141 TALD (Tactical Air Launched Decoy) missiles into the valley which prompted the Syrians' air defence systems to activate their search radars. Once the radar systems were activated they were quickly located by Israeli Tadiran Mastiff UAVs which relayed the information to IAI Scout UAVs operating well outside missile range. The information was then transmitted to E-2C Hawkeye aircraft operating off the coast and the sites were systematically destroyed by Israeli aircraft-launched AGM-78 and 45 anti-radiation missiles. Within just two hours the innovative tactics and technology of the Israeli Defence Forces had destroyed a total of seventeen out of nineteen surface-to-air-missile (SAM) batteries along with twenty-nine Syrian aircraft. By the time the Beqaa Valley War was over a total of twenty-nine of the Syrian SAM sites, along with ninety

The Israeli Aircraft Industries first and second generation unmanned aerial vehicles (UAVs) Scout (Zahavan) and Hunter (Hogla) are now classified as relics of the past. Today there is absolutely no doubt that UAVs revolutionize real-time intelligence. The Old Lady (Kshisha) of the IAI fleet, No. 401, is depicted in this July 1992 photograph undergoing Scheduled Depot Level Maintenance (SDLM) at IAI Malat plant. (O. Zidon Collection)

Syrian aircraft had been destroyed. The Israelis' carefully planned and executed Operation MOLE CRICKET 19 totally devastated the Russian High Command.

Like all modern weapon systems the UAV has continued to evolve not only in technology but mission requirements. The early UAVs of the Zroa Ha'Avir Ve'Halalal have been replaced with technically superior Elbit Hermes 450 UAVs and the IAI Heron Shoval (Trail) UAVs; both saw extensive service in the Gaza Strip during Operation CAST LEAD.

During June 2007 the Palestinian Hamas Islamic movement was able to take political and military control of the Gaza Strip. The terrorist organization has long advocated the total destruction of the State of Israel. Hamas has used the Gaza Strip as a launching platform for countless mortar and rocket attacks against Israel.

In response to the continuing Hamas rocket attacks into southern Israel the Zroa Ha'Avir Ve'Halalal launched Operation CAST LEAD on Saturday 27 December 2008, a large-scale military offensive against Hamas military targets including government facilities, military headquarters, and paramilitary installations and weapons storage facilities within the Gaza Strip. The UAVs of the IASF, Elbit Hermes 450s and Shovals, played an instrumental role during the twenty-five days of Operation CAST LEAD (27 December 2008–21 January 2009).

The twenty-foot-long Elbit Hermes 450 is a medium-sized multi-payload UAV, capable of missions as long as twenty hours. With a thirty-four-foot-five-inch wingspan the 450 has an operational range of approximately 124 miles with an average speed of 109mph. During Operation CAST LEAD the Elbit Hermes was tasked with what have been described as tactical long-range endurance missions (reconnaissance, surveillance, communications relay, target recognition, and verification).

and low acoustic signature make it difficult to detect during its forty-hour-long missions.

While operating at altitudes above 30,000 feet the Heron is designed to carry multiple payloads and perform multiple missions, such as Communications Intelligence (COMINT), Signals Intelligence (SIGINT), Image Intelligence (IMINT) or Synthetic Aperture Radar Sensor (SAR) and is further capable of target acquisition and artillery adjustments in support of ground troops.

In 1999 the Hermes 450 (above) entered service with the IASF assigned to No. 166 Squadron, operating out of Palmachim Air Base south of Tel Aviv. The Hermes 450 with its many payload (sensors) configurations provides real-time information regarding enemy positions, rocket launch sites and other vital information in support of ground troops. Sources also suggest that the Hermes has been adapted to be used as an assault UAV. The combat configuration would include two Hellfire or two Rafael air-to-ground missiles.

The Israeli Aerospace Industry medium-altitude long-endurance Heron Shoval (Trail) UAV was constantly deployed during Operation CAST LEAD. The Heron Shoval is equipped with a wide variety of sensors, which have the capability to provide real-time information over the battlefield. The Heron's quiet engine

The Heron Shoval, like the Hermes 450, conducts its covert strategic reconnaissance and surveillance missions from No. 200 Squadron flying out of Palmachim Air Base. During Operation CAST LEAD the Heron Shoval with its endurance was able to provide constant real-time video images depicting the movements of Hamas. (O. Zidon Collection)

IAI Heron TP Eitan (Firm) Arrives

During December 2010 the newest UAV, IAI Heron TP Eitan (Firm), joined the UAV fleet of the IASF. Eitan has been designed as an all-weather capable, multi-payload, multi-mission unmanned aerial vehicle. The Eitan UAV is at present based out of Tel-Nof Air Base in central Israel.

An Eitan squadron Seren (Captain) is seated at the control console during an operational UAV mission. The UAV fleet operates from Tel Nof Air Base. The control console allows the operator to monitor all aspects of the UAV mission. The top screen displays the position of the UAV while the lower screens allow the operator to monitor vital flight information and to ensure that the UAV is preforming within the mission parameters. (O. Zidon Collection)

IAI Heron TP Eitan No. 102 of No. 210 Squadron of the IASF is shown parked on the tarmac at Tel Nof Air Force Base. Housed in the whale-like nose of the aircraft are radar/satellite communication (SatCon) antennae for extended range. Positioned under the nose of No. 102, just in front of the wheel, is the UAV camera system. Extending from the top of the fuselage is the external communication antenna. (O. Zidon Collection)

The Eitan squadron will be integrated with Nos. 166 and 200 Squadrons, both of which are based and operate from Palmachim Air Base. The Eitan has been designed to operate at or above 45,000 feet during thirty-six-hour-long missions and is equipped with an automatic take-off and landing (ATOL) system. The forty-six-foot-long UAV is powered by a Pratt & Whitney PT6A, 900 kW, 1,200hp rear-fuselage-mounted turboprop engine.

Attack and Assault Helicopter Squadrons

Attack Helicopters

I don't believe any other aircraft can be associated with Special Operations (SOps) like the helicopter. The helicopter first presented itself on the battlefields of the world during the Second World War. Nazi Germany was the first to deploy the helicopter in small numbers, for observation, transport, and medical evacuation. Fortunately, extensive bombing by the Allied forces prevented Germany from producing helicopters in large quantities during the war. However, after the war the helicopter continued to evolve and, during the Korean and Vietnam Wars, proved its military value in combat operations in South East Asia.

Specifications: Bell A-1F Modernized Cobra

Tzefa (Viper) (photo)

General Characteristics:
Crew: 2, one pilot, one co-pilot/gunner
Length: 53 feet
Height: 13 feet 6 inches
Rotor diameter: 44 feet
Maximum takeoff weight: 10,000 pounds
Fuselage length: 44 feet 7 inches
Stub wing span: 10 feet 4 inches
Maximum speed: 172mph
Range: 315 miles (274 nautical miles)
Service ceiling: 12,200 feet
Rate of climb: 1,620 feet/minute
Gun: 1 General Dynamics 20mm (0.787-inch) M197 3-barrelled Gatling gun
Rockets: Hydra 70 2.75-inch (70mm) rockets – 7 rockets mounted in the M261 launcher
Missiles: TOW missiles – 4 or 8 missiles mounted in two-missile launchers on each hardpoint

The most common use of the military helicopter during the Vietnam War, as well as many of the military operations in the Middle East, was the transporting of troops to and from the battlefield. Modern military helicopters can be modified or converted to perform many other missions, such as combat search and rescue (SAR), medical evacuation (MEDEVAC), airborne command post, and the transport of troops and supplies to the battlefield. Military helicopters have evolved further to meet design and mission requirements.

The Zroa Ha'Avir Ve'Halalal has adopted and deployed the helicopter successfully in many special operations. The Israelis maintain attack and assault helicopters in a complete state of combat readiness twenty-four hours a day. The principal attack and assault helicopters deployed are the AH-64A and AH-64D Apache Longbow (photo below), and the Bell A-1H Cobra. The first A-1H Tzefa (Viper) arrived at Palmachim Air Base during April 1975. There are now two combat A-1H Tzefa squadrons (Nos. 161 'Northern Cobra' Squadron and 160 'Southern Cobra'

Specifications: Boeing AH-64A/D Longbow

AH-64A/B Peten (Python)/Saraf (Serpent)

General Characteristics:
Length: 49 feet 5 inches
Height: 15 feet 3 inches
Rotor diameter: 48 feet
Maximum takeoff weight: 23,000 pounds
Fuselage length: 59 feet 5 inches
Maximum speed: 182mph
Cruise speed: 165mph
Range: 295 miles
Service ceiling: 21,000 feet
Rate of climb: 2,500 feet/minute
Guns: 1 X30 X 113mm M230 Chain gun with 1,200 rounds
Rockets: Hydra 70–70 mm and CRV 7 70mm air-to-ground rockets
Missiles: Typically AGM-114 Hellfire variants and AIM-92 Stinger may also be carried

Squadron), both of which operate out of Palmachim Air Base. The AH-64A Peten (Python) operates with No. 113 Squadron (The Hornet Squadron) out of Ramon Air Base, while the AH-64D Saraf (Serpent) operates with No. 190 Squadron ('Magic Torch' Squadron) which also deploys out of Ramon.

Tactical Assault Helicopters

CH-53 Yas'ur (Petrel)

The Sikorsky CH-53 Sea Stallions of the Israeli armed forces have been deployed successfully in many combat operations since being selected as the primary heavy-lift assault helicopter. In Israeli service the Sea Stallion is known as the Yas'ur 2005 Petrel. The CH-53 is capable of carrying out any number of missions from tactical troop deployments and search and rescue operations to transporting supply and equipment to front-line ground forces.

In 1969, during the War of Attrition (Operation ROOSTER 53), the CH-53 Yas'ur demonstrated its payload-carrying capacity when it landed deep in Egypt and conveyed a captured Soviet advanced radar system back to Israel. Since 1973 the CH-53 has been used to land and extract Sayeret commandos on raids deep into Lebanon and Syria.

The Sikorsky CH-53, like the one depicted, more than proved its worth in Operation ROOSTER 53 during the War of Attrition in 1969. In the course of the operation Israeli paratroopers descended on the radar site under the cover of darkness and overpowered the defences. The radar site equipment was prepared for transport and one CH-53 carried the communications caravans and radar antenna, while the second took the heavier four-ton radar itself. Both CH-53s made their way back across the Red Sea to Israeli controlled territory.

Specifications: Sikorsky CH-53 Sea Stallion

Yas'ur (Petrel)

General Characteristics:
Crew: Two (2) Pilots – One or more crew chiefs
Capacity: 38 combat troops (55 in alternative configuration) or 24 stretchers
Length: 88 feet 6 inches
Height: 24 feet 11 inches
Rotor diameter: 72 feet 2.8 inches
Empty weight: 23,628 pounds
Load weight: 33,500 pounds
Maximum takeoff weight: 42,000 pounds
Maximum speed: 196mph
Cruise speed: 173mph
Range: 540 nautical miles
Combat radius: 95 miles
Service ceiling: 16,750 feet
Rate of climb: 2,460 feet/minute
Two door-mounted .50 BMG XM218 machine guns; some have ramp mounted .50 BMG GAU-21 machine guns

Sikorsky UH-60/S-70 Blackhawk

Yanshuf (Owl)

The UH-60 Blackhawk is a four-bladed, twin-engine, medium-lift utility helicopter which replaced the Bell UH-1 Iroquois. The Yanshuf (Owl) first engaged in combat with No. 124 Squadron ('Rolling Sword' Squadron), during Operation GRAPES OF WRATH against the Hezbollah in southern Lebanon. The UH-60 with its versatility and ability to carry sixteen Hellfire missiles is an outstanding launch platform for the laser-guided anti-armour missile.

In December 2008 the Israelis completed testing on the prototype UH-60 armed Blackhawk. This in-flight photograph of the armed UH-60 Blackhawk shows some of the new features such as an electro-optical/infrared sensors payload and cannon. The new UH-60s will be able to locate and engage targets up to four miles away. (O. Zidon Collection)

Specifications: Sikorsky UH-60/S70 Blackhawk

Yanshuf (Owl)

General Characteristics:
Crew: 2 pilots (flight crew) with 2 crew chiefs/gunners
Capacity: 2,640 pounds of cargo internally, including 14 combat troops or 6 stretchers
Length: 64 feet 10 inches
Fuselage width: 7 feet 9 inches
Height: 16 feet 10 inches
Empty weight: 10,624 pounds
Load weight: 22,000 pounds
Maximum takeoff weight: 23,500 pounds
Maximum speed: 222mph
Cruise speed: 173mph
Combat radius: 320 nautical miles
Service ceiling: 19,000 feet
Rate of climb: 700 feet/minute
Guns: 2 x 7.62mm (0.30-inch) M240H machine guns
  2 x 7.62mm (0.30-inch) M134 mini-guns
  2 x .50-inch (12.7mm) GAU19 Gatling guns
Hardpoints: 4, 2 per ESSS stub wing and provision to carry a combination of:
  Rockets: 70mm (2.75-in) Hydra 70 rockets
  Missiles: 16 AGM-114 Hellfire laser-guided missiles
  Other: 7.62mm (0.30-inch) 20mm (0.78-inch) or 30mm (1.18-inch) M230 gunpods

Heavy Transport Wing of the Zroa Ha'Avir Ve'Halalal

Boeing 707 Re'em (Antelope)

The Zroa Ha'Avir Ve'Halalal Boeing 707 Re'em fleet was formerly known as the 'International' Squadron. The squadron now operates from Nevatim Air Base and is identified as the 'Desert Giant' Squadron.

Boeing 707 Re'em No. 264 flying in formation with a trio of F-15 Bazs from the 'Twin Tail' Squadron. Re'em 264 is pictured in the new tanker fleet camouflage scheme of overall dark grey. The 'Desert Giant' Squadron, with its 707 tankers, has on many occasions demonstrated the aircraft's ability to support the IASF combat missions. The modified tankers of the IASF can carry eighty-five tons of fuel for themselves or for transfer to mission aircraft. (O. Zidon Collection)

No words can depict adequately the magnitude or impact that the heavy transport aircraft of the IASF have had on special missions or clandestine operations carried out over the years. Much has been written about the special operations of the Israeli Defence Forces: Operation THUNDERBOLT (4 July 1976), the rescue mission into Entebbe, Uganda; Operation OPERA (7 June 1981), the destruction of the Iraqi nuclear reactor; Operation WOODEN LEG (1 October 1985), the raid on Tunisia; Operation ORCHARD (6 September 2007), the air strike on the Syrian nuclear target. The one thing that all of these operations have in common is that none could have been accomplished without the direct involvement and support of the heavy transport aircraft of the IASF. Aircraft like the 707 Re'em (Antelope) and C-130 Karnaf (Rhinoceros) were absolutely indispensable. The unique capabilities of the 707 Re'em allow it to deploy not only as an in-flight air refuelling platform, but also as a command and control aircraft to co-ordinate air and ground operations. The IASF is believed to have at least four Re'em aircraft that have operated in both the SIGINT and Electronic Countermeasures (ECM) roles.

Specifications: Boeing 707 Tanker

707 Re'em (Antelope)

General Characteristics:
Crew: 3 pilots – co-pilot and hook operator
Capacity: 37 passengers
Payload: 83,000 pounds
Length: 136 feet 3 inches
Wingspan: 130 feet 10 inches
Height: 41 feet 8 inches
Empty weight: 98,466 pounds
Load weight: 297,000 pounds
Useful load: 200, 000 pounds
Maximum takeoff weight: 322,000 pounds
Maximum speed: 580mph
Cruise speed: 530mph
Range: 1,500 miles with 150,000 pounds of transfer fuel
Service ceiling: 50,000 feet
Rate of climb: 4,900 feet/minute

Lockheed C-130-J-30 Hercules

Karnaf (Rhinoceros)

The Lockheed C-130 Hercules was designed as a four-turboprop-engine, fixed-wing military transport aircraft. The Hercules has been produced in over forty models and variants which have served with over sixty nations.

The aircraft was designed with the ability to use unprepared runways for take-off and landing. The C-130 was originally designed as a troop, medical evacuation and cargo transport aircraft. However, the versatility of the airframe has seen it adapted for a multitude of missions. Besides the transporting of seventy-two combat troops or sixty-four paratroopers, the aircraft can carry out a variety of other roles, including (AC-130) heavily armed ground attack, airborne assault, search and rescue, weather reconnaissance, aerial refuelling and tactical airlift.

The Lockheed C-130s of the Zroa Ha'Avir Ve'Halalal have a long and distinguished combat record. Without a doubt the Entebbe Raid into Uganda, in 1976, was one of the most spectacular missions ever carried out by C-130 aircrews of the IASF and at least two of the Rhinoceros deployed are still flying with combat units. No. 102 was the lead C-130 to land in Uganda during the Entebbe Raid and No. 420, which also took part in the raid, was also involved in Operation SOLOMON which brought over 15,000 Ethiopian Jews to Israel during one weekend in 1991.

The Israelis are now looking to replace many of the ageing Rhinoceros with the newer Lockheed Super Hercules C-130-J-30

The Lockheed C-130H Karnaf was originally designed and built as a troop and cargo transport aircraft. During its fifty-five years of continuous production the Hercules has continued to prove its versatility as a gunship (AC-130), airborne assault, search and rescue (SAR) and aerial refuelling tanker. The C-130 has become the main tactical airlift aircraft of many air forces the world over. This particular C-130 Karnaf of the 'Yellow Bird' Squadron demonstrates its supply-dropping capabilities. (O. Zidon Collection)

Specifications: Lockheed C-130-J-30 Super Hercules

Shimshon (Samson)

General Characteristics:
Capacity: 128 passengers
   92 airborne troops
   97 litter patients – 2 medical personnel
   8 pallets
Payload: 44,000 pounds
Length: 112 feet 9 inches
Height: 38 feet 10 inches
Empty weight: 75,562 pounds
Useful load: 72,000 pounds
Maximum takeoff weight: up to 175,000 pounds
Maximum speed: 417mph
Cruse speed: 400mph
Range: 3,262 miles
Service ceiling: Absolute altitude 40,386 feet
Take-off distance: 3,127 feet

models. The Israeli Super Hercules will be known as the Shimshon (Samson, the Jewish biblical hero equivalent of the Greek mythological hero Hercules). The newer Super Hercules C-130-J-30 will be equipped with four Rolls Royce AE2100DB turboprop engines, with new composite scimitar propellers, and a new flight deck equipped with digital avionics.

Chapter Twelve

The Sounds of War Growing Louder

With the end of the Yom Kippur War (6–25 October 1973) signs began to appear that the status quo in the Middle East may have been broken at long last. In 1978 Egypt and Israel signed the Camp David Accords, which resulted in the 26 March 1979 Peace Treaty between the former enemies. The treaty, signed by President Anwar El Sadat and Israeli Prime Minister Menachem Begin, ended the state of war that had existed since 1948. Egypt thus became the first Arab State officially to recognize Israel. However, the signing of the treaty caused controversy across the Arab World, and was a contributing factor in the assassination of President Sadat at the annual victory parade in Cairo on 6 October 1981.

On 26 October 1984 Jordan became the second Arab country to enter into a peace treaty with Israel, ending the state of war that had existed between Jordan and Israel since 1948.

It was hoped that the Middle Eastern peace process would have a profound effect on Israel by removing two former enemies from the order of battle. It is true that the treaties have endured but they have not brought an end to hostilities in the Middle East. During the 1991 Gulf War Iraq fired at least eighty-eight SCUD missiles at Coalition forces and Israel. With the events in the Middle East today, Iran's nuclear ambitions and unrest in the Arab world the sounds of war grow louder once again in the Middle East.

With the hate-filled rhetoric that comes from Iran and its radical terrorist proxy groups almost daily, it is little wonder that Israel views Iran as a real threat, citing frequent Iranian calls for the destruction of Israel. Iran, its Hezbollah allies in Lebanon, and Hamas militants in Gaza, have all stated that their ultimate goal is the annihilation of Israel. The Iranians, Syrians, Hezbollah, Hamas, the Muslim Brotherhood and other fanatical Muslim groups have always hated the Israelis and Americans.

Most of the world, particularly Israel, is convinced that Iran's quest to capture the atom is for the development of nuclear weapons, and not for peaceful uses as claimed by the Iranians. Due to the sensitive nature of the nuclear programmes in Iran the government has placed a great deal of censorship and secrecy around those programmes in order to protect the military applications of their nuclear activities.

There is every likelihood that the regime hardliners in Tehran intend to develop nuclear weapons and ballistic missile technology. The fanatical Islamist regime in Tehran has gone to great lengths to protect these programmes. Nuclear sites have been located purposely throughout the country, with many of the more sensitive or important sites (Fordow and Natanz) in underground bunkers. These important sites are defended strongly with surface-to-air missiles and radar controlled anti-aircraft weapons. There is also evidence that upgraded SAMs have been supplied to many Middle

Eastern countries, including Iran. The Iranians have no shortage of technology partners, such as North Korea, India, China, and Russia, all of whom are supplying not only weapons technology, but the weapons themselves to Iran. Great concern has been expressed by the International Atomic Energy Agency (IAEA) that the nuclear uranium enrichment programmes in Iran may be a precursor to the building and production of nuclear weapons by the regime.

The United Nations and the world community at large have attempted to establish a dialogue, and a policy of sanctions, with and against Iran. The attempts at dialogue and sanctions have had no effect on the Iranians, and have allowed the regime to continue their stalling tactics thus enabling them to pursue their nuclear ambitions. The persistent stonewalling by the Iranians is reminiscent of North Korea: dialogue, sanctions, dialogue and more sanctions; in the end the world wakes up, and discovers the North Koreans have the bomb. The Israelis are truly concerned, and justifiably so, that the same outcome awaits the Middle East, and they are not willing to accept the risk that presents itself when Iran has the capability to produce nuclear weapons and the ballistic missiles to deliver them.

The latest intelligence coming from the Middle East indicates that Iran, Syria, Hezbollah, and Hamas may have as many as 200,000 rockets, mortars and missiles aimed at Israel. The threat of the Islamist fanatics in Tehran having nuclear weapons is a tangible and real one to the State of Israel.

Middle East Ablaze

The threat to Israel is real and much more tangible than the world's liberal media and the fanatic Islamist regimes in the Middle East will admit. History in the Middle East demonstrates that the fanatics from Tehran, Syria, Hezbollah, Hamas and the PLO don't need an excuse to kill Israelis; they have always been able to excuse acts of violence against not only the Israelis, but others who don't subscribe to their fanatical doctrine. These fanatical groups will not rest until they have destroyed what they believe are the infidel cultures of the world, and imposed their totalitarian enslavement on anything or anyone who challenges their belief systems.

The hardliners in Tehran are underestimating the Israeli state's capability to deal a significant and unbelievably ferocious blow to the Iranian nuclear weapons programmes. Even retired Admiral Mike Mullen, Chairman of the US Joint Chiefs, has raised doubts that Israel could carry out such a mission on its own. Don't bet against the Israelis! A pre-emptive air strike against Iran is not going to be easy and is not for the timid. However, the Israeli Air Force has always demonstrated great ingenuity and skill in penetrating its enemies' air defence systems. If the Israelis decide to launch a pre-emptive air strike against Iran's nuclear facilities it will be with a devastating Israeli onslaught. The Iranian response to the air strike will at best be unpredictable. What is predictable will be the firestorm of criticism, censure, and ridicule that will follow against Israel.

'Yes We Can!'

'Yes We Can!' Major General (Reserve) Eitan Ben Eliyahu stated unequivocally that Israeli military armed forces have the capability to take out Iran's nuclear weapons installations. The former Commander of the Heyl Ha'Avir was quoted recently as stating 'we have been training for it, we have the aircraft and the pilots and we can fulfil the mission day or night and in all weather conditions'. The Zroa Ha'Avir Ve'Halalal is constantly training for all aspects of combat air operation. Training not only involves IASF units but foreign forces like the Luftwaffe at Decimomannu in Sardinia, the Turkish Air Force, the United Kingdom's Royal Air Force, Italy's Aeronautica Militare and the United States Air Force. These training exercises have given the IASF the ability to engage in air-to-air combat profiles against front-line aircraft as well as long range training missions. Other sources indicate that Israeli front-line air units are not only training for but have systematically built up their capabilities specifically for a possible air strike against Iranian nuclear facilities. The Israelis realized that a major obstacle that has to be overcome in any pre-emptive strike will be the midair refuelling of their strike aircraft. During 2008 the Israelis approached the Bush administration in an attempt to obtain KC-135 tankers and deep penetration GBU-28 bunker-buster bombs, which were delivered in 2009. Sources also stated that the Israelis have requested the BLU-118/B thermobaric bomb, also known as Big Blue Two. The BLU-118/B has a penetrating warhead filled with advanced thermobaric explosives. The weapon is quite effective when detonated within a tunnel, or underground bunkers. At the time the US denied the request.

In September 2011 Fox News quoted an Israeli news source: 'US offered Israelis advanced weaponry in exchange for delay in Iran attack. The mounting evidence suggests that plans already exist for a pre-emptive strike on Iranian targets.'

The principal nuclear sites in Iran (of which there are ten) include Isfahan, Qom and Natanz. The Russians plan to deliver, or have delivered, fuel to the Busheher power station which is a mere 973 miles from Tel Aviv. An air strike on the nuclear power station at Busheher could lead to the leaking of radioactive material, a major threat in itself, which has to be considered.

Should Israel strike at Iran the problems facing them are many although the distance from Tel Aviv to Tehran is only 1,000 miles; the geographical situation places not only Tehran but nuclear sites like Busheher within range of the IASF. Tel Aviv's close proximity to Tehran and a number of nuclear sites will not eliminate one of the major hurdles facing the IASF in any pre-emptive strike. The Israeli ability to refuel the strike force will be tested. Not only will the limited number of tankers available be a problem, but the slow, vulnerable tankers, lacking manoeuvrability, will be a priority target for Iranian fighters.

If the order is finally given the Zroa Ha'Avir Ve'Halalal will play the lead role. Support aircraft will be launched from air bases throughout Israel – refuelling tankers from the 'Desert Giant' Squadron, search and rescue units (SAR), air combat aircraft and air defence suppression aircraft.

The F-15I Ra'ams and F-16I Sufas will be fuelled and armed, pilots and ground crews at their posts. The customary bantering between pilots will have stopped. Pilots and ground crews will be alert and silent, poised to act. The strike force will begin taxiing to the last chance point where weapons will be armed, and last minute inspections of the aircraft made. Crew chiefs and weapons troops will be rapidly falling back as the ferociousness of the Israeli Air Forces is set in motion. All thoughts will then be about accomplishing their missions.

Si vis pacem, para bellum
(If you want peace, prepare for war)

The United Nations (UN) has proven unequal to the task of dealing with Iran's nuclear ambitions. Islamist radicalism continues to preach the destruction of the State of Israel, and the time of uncertainty, unpredictable, and doubt as to what course to pursue may have passed.

The Israeli ordnance crews have completed the loading of bombs and missiles. The crew chiefs and mechanics have checked and re-checked their aircraft, for the success of the mission may hinge largely on their efforts. The F-15I Ra'ams and F-16I Sufas are parked on flight lines with full weapon loads throughout Israel. Soon those flight lines will be alive; the noise of the jet engines, warm gusts of jet exhaust fumes, the familiar smell of burning jet fuel will fill the air. And once again the air force jets of Israel will prepare to thunder down runways ready to get airborne, hoping to penetrate the air defence systems of Iran and deliver a catastrophic blow to the nuclear weapons programmes of the Iranians.

Israeli Front-Line Combat Aircraft

I don't think it's a matter of *if* but more of *when* will the Zroa Ha'Avir Ve'Halalal launch a pre-emptive air strike against Iran's nuclear weapons sites. The main Israeli strike force will be deployed from air bases (Ramat David, Hatzor, Hatzerim, Tel Nof, Ovdu and Ramon) throughout Israel. The high-end strike force will be made up of the F-15I Ra'am and the F-16I Sufa strike aircraft. The F-15Is of the 'Hammer' Squadron, and F-16I Squadrons have all been modified to carry Israeli electronic warfare, radars, munitions, and command and control systems for deep-penetration missions. Additional assets for any pre-emptive strike will be drawn from other Israeli F-15 and F-16 squadrons.

The F-15I Ra'ams, and F-16I Sufas in this collection of photographs will be many of the very aircraft and weapons systems tasked to face the ferocious and tenacious Iranian air defences in any strike on nuclear facilities within Iran.

A scary sight of an F-16I Sufa emerging from a hardened shelter displaying a mighty ordnance configuration of both offensive and defensive weapons. I'm not quite sure what caught the eye of the photographer; the sleek lines of the Sufa or the graceful and sleek lines of the ground crew who gently manoeuvre the jet out of its shelter for an operational mission. (O. Zidon Collection)

'Negev' Squadron F-16I No. 253 is seen silhouetted against a brilliant desert sunset at its home base at Ramon. The aircraft is pictured taxiing from the last chance point prior to take-off, and is heavily armed for a combat mission. This 'Negev' Squadron jet is configured with two American made AIM-120 AAMs along with two Rafael Python 5 air-to-air missiles. In this image No. 253 is carrying two GBU-15 glide bombs, used to destroy high value enemy targets. The GBU-15 has a low-to-medium altitude delivery with pinpoint accuracy. (O. Zidon Collection)

F-16I No. 253 from the 'Negev' Squadron stands ready for take-off with its heavy load of offensive and defensive weapons. The GBU-15s on the centre wing hardpoints are MK-84 general purpose or BLU-109s with penetrating warheads. Communications, navigation and targeting pods are located on the centreline hardpoints. This photograph may very well have been taken during Operation CAST LEAD in December 2008. The first wave of attack aircraft during that operation were intended to carry out sixty-four sorties against fifty Hamas targets. (O. Zidon Collection)

'Negev' Squadron F-16I No. 422 is heavily armed with two GBU-10 bombs, two AIM-120 air-to-air missiles on the wingtips and two Rafael Python-4 air-to-air missiles on wing hardpoints. With its conformal and wing fuel tanks the F-16I is able to extend its combat range. (O. Zidon Collection)

The summer sun is setting at Ramon AB as F-16I 882 of the 'One' Squadron prepares to launch during Operation CAST LEAD. On Saturday 27 December 2008 the Israelis launched the operation into the Gaza Strip, which has long been the source of mortar, shelling and rocket attacks against Israel. Sufa 882 is configured for an air-to-ground mission carrying two GBU-10 Paveway II laser-guided bombs (smart bombs). (O. Zidon Collection)

F-16I Sufa aircraft of the Zroa Ha'Avir Ve'Halalal are prepared at air bases all over Israel for a quick reaction launch. The F-16I Sufa in this image is being readied for an air-to-ground mission. The aircraft is armed with two JDAM GPS guided bombs, along with two AIM-9L Sidewinder air-to-air missiles. If the order is given to strike at Iran's nuclear weapons facilities the F-16I Sufa with its extended range will be among the first attack aircraft over the target. (O. Zidon Collection)

F-15I Ra'am No. 244 is on final approach, gear down, flaring its nose for landing. The F-15Is of the 'Hammer' Squadron are classified as the Zroa Ha'Avir Ve'Halalal premier multi-purpose fighters. The Ra'ams of the 'Hammer' Squadron are usually heavily armed with bombs or air-to-ground missiles. However, in this unusual photograph of No. 244, the aircraft is armed for an air-to-air mission and configured with four Rafael Python and two AIM-7 Sparrow air-to-air missiles. (O. Zidon Collection)

A two-seat 'Bat' Squadron F-16I 451 Sufa takes off in full power from Ramon Air Base on a training sortie. Sufa 451 was part of the first batch of F-16Is received under the Peace Marble V contract. The new tail art of the 'Bat' Squadron has retained the red chevron denoting the historical past of the squadron. The red chevron can be traced back to the squadron's days as a Mirage CJ III unit. (O. Zidon Collection)

F-16C Barak No. 558 from the 'First Fighter' Squadron utilizes brute force in a full afterburner take-off to gain altitude. On any pre-emptive strike into Iran the strike aircraft will be protected by the F-16s and F-15s configured similarly to the Barak in this photograph. Located on the wingtips are two AIM-9L Sidewinder heat-seeking air-to-air missiles. The aircraft also carries two Python 5 air-to-air missiles. (O. Zidon Collection)

F-15I Ra'am No. 252 operates from Hatzerim Air Base, home of the 'Hammer' Squadron. Unlike F-15I No. 244 in a previous photograph, F-15I No. 252 is depicted with a unique asymmetric weapons load. On the starboard side of the aircraft are three GBU-10 bombs with a fourth GBU-10 on the centreline pylon. On the port-side pylons are six GP bombs. The 'Hammer' Squadron tail art on 252 is much larger and far more impressive than the initial 2001 art work. (O. Zidon Collection)

The F-15B Baz has always been the main air superiority fighter of the Zroa Ha'Avir Ve'Halalal. However, like most weapon systems in Israel, the Baz has undergone many modifications. F-15B No. 408 in this picture demonstrates the air-to-ground capabilities that have been added to the Baz. The F-15B in the IASF is now capable of carrying both JDAM and Rafael Popeye munitions as is evident in this photograph of No. 408 of the 'Twin Tail' Squadron. (IDF photo via O. Zidon Collection)

The double MiG killer No. 848, which carries the nickname Nesher, meaning Eagle, is configured with both air-to-ground and air-to-air weapons. Located under each wing and centreline hardpoints are three JDAM bombs. For self-defence Baz 848 is armed with two Rafael Python-3 heat-seeking air-to-air missiles. No. 848 claimed two aerial combat victories (one MiG-21 and one Gazelle) during June 1982. (O. Zidon Collection)

This F-15D from the 'Spearhead' Squadron is parked on the tarmac with a heavy ordnance load. Baz 979 is armed with one Rafael Popeye tucked under one wing while tucked under the opposite wing are three Rafael Python-3 air-to-air missiles, and one fuel tank. Located on the centreline hardpoint is the Popeye communication pod. Baz 979 has been credited with downing three MiGs, one MiG-21 and two MiG-23s, in air-to-air combat during June 1982. (O. Zidon Collection)

This 'One' Squadron F-15I is taking off on full power using its afterburner to gain speed and altitude. The Sufa is a lightweight and highly manoeuvrable fighter with the ability to carry both air-to-air and air-to-ground weapons. Sufa No. 854 is configured with AIM-120 AAM and Python 5 AAM for self-defence after completing its air-to-ground mission. (O. Zidon Collection)

Two unusual views of 'Hammer' Squadron F-15I Ra'am heavily armed with two Popeye cruise missiles. The single-stage solid-fuel rocket can deliver a 750lb blast/ fragmentation or 800lb penetrating warhead on its targets with a great degree of accuracy. (O. Zidon Collection)

In three minutes and forty seconds the Zroa Ha'Avir Ve'Halalal launched sixty-four combat sorties into the Gaza Strip. The first wave placed over 100 tons of bombs and missiles on fifty terrorist targets. Heavily armed and with brute force F-16I 890 of the 'One' Squadron departs from Ramon Air Base in full afterburner. The aircraft is armed with two AIM-120 and two Rafael Python 5 air-to-air missiles along with two Delilah air-to-ground missiles. (O. Zidon Collection)

The F-16C/D Barak , like No. 088 in this photograph, entered service with the Zroa Ha'Avir Ve'Halalal in 1987. The 'Valley' Squadron Barak fleet includes both the single-seat and two-seat aircraft. Like most aircraft in the Isreali inventory the Barak continues to undergo modifications in avionics, communication and weapons capabilities. In this view No. 088 is fully armed with both air-to-air and air-to-ground weapons. (O. Zidon Collection)

The two F-16I Sufas captured in this photograph are deployed with the 'One' Squadron. This particular photograph was featured on the cover of Ofer Zidon and Shlomo Aloni's book, Israeli Air Force, Cutting Edge, *and may have been taken during Operation CAST LEAD in December 2008. It was on the 27th that Israel began launching air strikes against the Palestinian Hamas Islamic movement in the Gaza Strip. Both F-16Is are armed with a full complement of GBU-10 bombs and AIM-120 and Rafael Python 5 air-to-air missiles. (O. Zidon Collection)*

Weapons and Technology

IASF front-line F-16I and F-15I combat aircraft of today, like their predecessors, will soon join the Ouragans, Mystères, Mirages, Neshers and Phantoms on the long list of of relics of the past. Until then the the F-15Is and F-16Is of the IASF will stand ready for every battle, every mission as the photographs in the Special Mission and Israeli front-line combat aircraft section demonstrate.

The Zroa Ha'Avir Ve'Halalal is presently establishing its operational requirements to update its front-line combat aircraft. In order for the Israelis to maintain their air supremacy in the Middle East they are formulating requirements to obtain new fifth generation aircraft and weapons.

The IASF, with its civilian authority, have entered into negotiations with the United States to obtain the Lockheed Martin F-35 Lightning II. The Israelis hope to purchase between seventy-five and one hundred of the new stealth fighters. Regarding the F-35 Lightning II, one high-ranking Israeli official is quoted in the *Jerusalem Post* as saying 'The F-35 could be over Tehran before they even know it's there'. In keeping with its modernization programme the Israelis have also made overtures to the United States' Department of Defense in an attempt to obtain a hundred Lockheed Martin F-22 Raptors. Unfortunately for the Israelis, the F-22 Raptor, with its unique stealth and beyond visual range (BVR) air combat capabilities, is protected by United States' law from export to other countries. If and when an export version of the Raptor is authorized the IASF will probably be the first nation to obtain the aircraft.

If the attempts to obtain the Lockheed Martin F-35 falter, the Israelis, who have a close defence relationship with Italy, may seek to obtain the Eurofighter. Another option being pursued is the stealth-enhanced F-15SE (Silent Eagle), which is reported to have a longer range, and a wider set of integrated weapons systems.

The IASF has always demonstrated a rich seam of innovation in its modernization of its aircraft. That modernization is not limited only to aircraft, but includes the air-to-air and air-to-ground weapons deployed by the force. The day of the unguided weapon in the IASF is all but over. Today's air warfare requires precision-guided attack and tactical missiles. The Zroa Ha'Avir Ve'Halalal continues to upgrade not only aircraft but, weapons like the Delilah and Have Nap cruise missiles. Air-to-air combat has always captured our imagination although the IASF mission has always been to project enough firepower in the battle space to support its ground and naval forces.

During Operation PILLAR of DEFENCE (14–21 November 2012) the IASF successfully deployed one of Israel's newest innovations, the new mobile all-weather air defence system, Iron Dome. Operated by the Zroa Ha'Avir Ve'Halalal Iron Dome is designed to intercept and destroy short range-rockets and artillery shells and was credited with its first successful intercept on 7 April 2011 when it destroyed a Grad rocket launched from Gaza. Iron Dome was declared operational and deployed on 27 March 2011.

The Iron Dome system has three central components (Detection and Tracking Radar; Battle Management and Weapon Control (BMC) centre; Missile Firing Unit) and is designed and built to identify and intercept only those rockets that are threats to populated areas. The missile firing unit is equipped with twenty interceptor Tamir missiles; each battery contains sixty missiles. Zroa Ha'Ve'Halalal Iron Dome batteries are credited with destroying 400-plus rockets fired at Israel during Operation PILLAR of DEFENCE.

The Israelis will soon be fielding a new air defence system to be deployed and used in conjunction with the Iron Dome system. The new system, known as David's Sling or Magic Wand, will be operational sometime in 2013 or 2014. David's Sling is designed to intercept medium-to-long-range rockets or cruise missiles, such as those possessed by Hezbollah. The interceptor missile of David's Sling is referred to as Stunner, a fire-and-forget two-stage missile.

The Zroa Ha'Avir Ve'Halalal has not restricted its innovation and modernization to its aircraft and weapons systems. As a direct result of the Yom Kippur War it became clear that the IASF needed the ability and capability to independently collect aerial intelligence. In 1977 the ultra secret ISTAR (Intelligence, Surveillance, Target Acquisition and Reconnaissance) unit was formed. What is known about the unit is that it is dispersed throughout Israel and consists of a ground element, which collects intelligence regarding specific areas, and an airborne element that collects information using the most modern aircraft, UAVs and satellites. The information from both elements is processed to produce useable intelligence which is passed to relevant commands. Though not publicly acknowledged it is a safe bet that ISTAR has been a principal element in Operations CAST LEAD and PILLAR of DEFENCE.

Epilogue

On or about 18 December 2010 events in the Middle East brought a glimmer of hope that change was under way in the region and across North Africa. What has become known as the Arab Spring (Arab Awakening or Arab Uprisings) movement erupted throughout the Middle East, contributing to revolution, demonstration, protest and civil wars in the Arab world. Leaders from Tunisia, (Zin El Abidine Ben Ali) Egypt (Hosni Mubarak), Libya (Muammar Gaddafi) and Yemen (Ali Abdulla Saleh) have been forced from power. Protests have broken out in at least twelve other Arab countries with the most violent being in Syria.

In the first Egyptian election since the Mubarak government was forced from power a member of the Muslim Brotherhood has been elected president of Egypt. The Muslim Brotherhood is the most influential and largest movement in the Middle East. In a very close election, the Muslim Brotherhood's Mohamed Morsi assumed the office of the Presidency of Egypt. Within days of assuming power the Muslin Brotherhood declared that the peace treaty with Israel will be revised or cancelled.

During November 2012, in response to continued rocket attacks in southern Israel, the Zroa Ha'Avir Ve'Halalal was ordered to locate and eliminate Ahmed Jabari, Chief of the Gaza Military Wing of Hamas. This mission was accomplished on 14 November 2012 when an IASF missile struck a vehicle in which Jabari was a passenger. The assassination of Jabari brought an immediate response from Gaza militants. Rockets and mortars rained down on Israel. The Israelis retaliated much as they did in December 2008 when they engaged in a three-week conflict (Operation CAST LEAD) with militants in Gaza. From 14 to 21 November 2012 the Israelis conducted Operation PILLAR of DEFENCE against Hamas and Palestinian militants. During the twelve days of Operation PILLAR of DEFENCE hundreds of Iranian Fajr-5 and Russian Grad and Katyusha rockets were launched against Israel which caused little damage although three Israelis were killed in Kiryat Malachi.

On 21 November 2012 a ceasefire was announced between Hamas and Israel which, in effect, halted Israeli operations in Gaza. To date nothing has been resolved in Gaza or the Middle East generally. As always in the Middle East, any ceasefire, treaty or agreement can change easily and very quickly for the worst.

Within days of the ceasefire between Israel and Hamas, which was brokered by Egypt, the Egyptian President, Mohammed Morsi, sent the Egyptian people back onto the streets. Morsi and the Muslim Brotherhood announced to the world an extraordinary set of new presidential powers giving him unchecked powers.

When discussing the Middle East the old adage of 'the more things change the more they stay the same' remains true. Israel is surrounded by Arab states that seem bent on destroying her. Regarding peace between Israel and her Arab neighbours there are two quotes, attributed to the late Prime Minister of Israeli, Golda Meir, which are quite profound: 'Peace will come when Arabs will love their children more than they hate us.' 'No Alternative. The Egyptians could run to Egypt, the Syrians into Syria. The only place we could run was into the sea, and before we did that we might as well *fight*.'

Glossary of Terms and Abbreviations

AA	Air-to-air (weapon)
AAA	Anti-aircraft artillery
AAM	Air-to-air missile
Acft	Aircraft
ACM	Air combat manoeuvring
ACT	Air combat tactics
ADF	Air Defence Force
AGL	Above ground level
AGM	Air-to-ground missile
Ahit	Eagle (Hebrew) Israeli name for the Douglas A-4 Skyhawk
AIM	Air-launched interceptor missile
AIM-9	Sidewinder air-to-air missile, passive infra-red type (B, C, D, E, G, J, L and M models)
AIM-7	Sparrow air-to-air missile, semi-active radar type
AIM-120	AMRAAM – Advanced Medium Range Air-to-Air Missile
Air abort	Cancellation of an aircraft's mission for any reason other than enemy action, at any time from take-off to mission completion
AI	Airborne interception radar
Angle-off	Angular position off the tail of the reference aircraft
AOB	Air Order of Battle
ARM	Anti-radiation missile

ASM	Air-to-surface missile
Aspect angle	The angular measurement between the line of sight, in degrees
Atoll	Soviet-built air-to-air missile, infra-red seeker type, similar to US AIM-9 IR-homing missile
Auto-track	Automatic tracking in which a servo-mechanism keeps the radar beam trained on the target
AW	Automatic weapons
AWACS	Airborne Warning and Control System
Ballistic	Unguided, i.e. follows a ballistic trajectory when thrust is terminated
Bandit	An enemy aircraft
Barak	F-16 C/D Fighting Falcon (Lightning) in Israeli service
BARCAP	Barrier combat air patrol; fighter cover between the strike force and an area of expected threat; a MiG screen for one or more missions
Baz	F-15 A/D/C/D Eagle in Israeli service
Blip	(radar) A spot of light on a radar scope, representing the relative position of a reflecting object such as an aircraft
Bogey	Unidentified aircraft
Bogies	Two or more unidentified aircraft

Break   An emergency turn in which maximum performance is desired instantly to destroy an attacker's tracking solution of intercepting and destroying hostile aircraft before they reach their target

BVR   Beyond Visual range

CAOPC   Combined Air Operations Centre

CAP   Combat air patrol; an aircraft patrol provided over an objective area, over the force

Centreline tank   a fuel tank carried externally on the centreline of the aircraft

Chaff   thin, narrow metallic strips of various lengths to provide different responses, used to create false signals on radar scopes

Close   To decrease separation between aircraft

Closure   Relative closing velocity

Col   Colonel

Combat-spread   A loose formation which affords each flight member the opportunity for maximum visual look-out

Capt   Captain

CR   Credit or aerial victory

Cut-off (tactic)   Employing the shortest route to intercept an enemy airborne target

Deck   A flight altitude just above the surface, as used in such phrases as 'to hit the deck', 'to fly on the deck' and to 'dive toward the deck'

DCA   Defensive Counter Air

Defensive split   A descending, accelerating dive using high-G while continuing to roll to negate an attack and gain lateral separation

Delilah   Air-to-surface Israeli developed cruise missile

Deploy   To relocate forces to desired areas of operation

Disengage   To break off combat with the enemy

DF   Direction finding

Dogfight   An aerial battle, especially between opposing fighters, involving considerable manoeuvring and violent aerobatics on both sides

EAF   Egyptian Air Force

Eagle   McDonnell Douglas (now Boeing) F-15 fighter

Echelon   A formation in which flight members are staggered sequentially on one side of the lead aircraft

ECM   Electronic countermeasures: the prevention or reduction of effectiveness in enemy equipment and tactics used by electromagnetic radiations; some exploit the enemy's emissions of these radiations

ECM pod   Pylon- or fuselage-mounted container which houses multiple transmitters and associated electronic devices; a self-protection device for aircraft penetrating an electronically-controlled ground-to-air defence system

Element   USAF term for the basic fighting unit (two aircraft)

Encounter   A series of time-continuous actions between specific friendly and enemy aircraft

Engagement   An encounter which involves hostile or aggressive action by one or more of the participants

EW   Electronic warfare

EWO   Electronic warfare officer

FAC   Forward Air Controller

Faceplate   North Atlantic Treaty Organization (NATO) designator for early models of the MiG-21

Falcon   General Dynamics (now Lockheed Martin) F-16 fighter

Farmer   NATO designator for the MiG-19

Fast CAP Combat air patrol for strike aircraft, particularly fighters, as opposed to slow CAP

1st Lt (or 1Lt) First Lieutenant

Fishbed NATO designator for later models of the MiG-21

Fitter NATO designator for the Sukhoi Su-22

Flak Anti-aircraft fire

Flak envelope A varying vertical unit of airspace in which a particular type of AAA is effective

Flight a tactical fighter unit, usually consisting of two elements, each element of two aircraft

FLIR Forward looking infra-red

Flogger NATO designator for the MiG-23

FOB Forward operating base

FORCAP Force combat air patrol: patrol of fighters maintained over task force to destroy enemy aircraft which might threaten

Foxbat NATO designator for the MiG-25

Fresco NATO designator for the MiG-17

Ftr Abbreviation for fighter

G Unit of acceleration: unit of force applied to a body at rest equal to the force exerted on it by gravity

Gaggle A number of aircraft operating in close proximity but not necessarily in any semblance of formation

GBU Guided Bomb Unit

GCA Ground controlled approach

GCI Ground controlled interception

GPS Global positioning system

Growl See missile tone

Guide (air-to-air missile) to follow the course intended when fired

Heat Armament switch setting for using infra-red missile

Harrier BAE Systems (formerly Hawker-Siddeley) short/vertical take-off attack/fighter aircraft

HAS Hardened aircraft shelter

Have Nap Israeli developed air-to-surface cruise missile

HEI High explosive incendiary

High-G Status of having the G-load increased during aircraft manoeuvring

Hos(ed) (ing) To direct an intense stream of gunfire toward the target, sometimes by pulling lead and allowing the enemy aircraft to fly into it

HUD Head-Up display

IAS Indicated air speed

IASF Israeli Air and Space Force

ID Identification

IDF/AF Israeli Defence Force/Air Force

IFF Identification, Friend or Foe: aircraft transponding beacon receiver radar information distinguishing friend from foe

IFR In-flight refuelling

IP Initial point; a well-defined point, usually distinguishable visually and/or by radar, used as a starting point for a bomb run to a target or for other tactical purposes, such as air refuelling

IR Infra-red

IR missile An infra-red (heat-seeking) missile

Iron Dome Mobile all weather air defence system

JCS Joint Chiefs of Staff (United States)

JDAM Joint direct attack munitions

Jink(ed) (ing) Constant manoeuvring in both the horizontal and vertical planes to present a difficult target to enemy defences by spoiling the tracking solution: a

	simultaneous change in bank, pitch, and velocity at random	**MiG**	Soviet/Russian aircraft from the Mikoyan-Gurevich design bureau
Judy	Term used to indicate that the interceptor has contact with the target and is assuming control of the engagement	**MiGCAP (or MiG cap)**	Combat air patrol directed specifically against MiG aircraft
KCAS	Knots calibrated air speed	**Military power**	Maximum unaugmented (no afterburner) thrust of the aircraft engine
KIAS	Knots indicated air speed	**Missile free**	Authority to fire missiles unless a target is identified as friendly
Kill	An enemy aeroplane shot down or otherwise destroyed by military action while in flight	**Missile tone**	Audio signal indicating an AIM-9 is locked on to an infra-red source
Kt	Knot (one nautical mile per hour)	**M-61**	Vulcan 20mm cannon
KTAS	Knots true air speed	**M/Sgt**	Master Sergeant
Kurnass	F-4E Phantom II in IDF/AF service (Sledgehammer)	**MSL**	Mean sea level, used as a reference for altitude
Lead(er)	The lead aircraft in a flight or element, or the lead element of a flight; also a reference to a specific lead aircraft or its pilot	**Narrow Gate**	Mode which can be selected on a radar missile which will allow it to home only on targets with selected range of 'rate of closure'
Lethal envelope	The envelope within which parameters can be met for successful employment of a munition by a particular weapons system	**Netz**	Sparrowhawk: F-16A/B Fighting Falcon in Israeli service
LGB	Laser-guided bomb	**NM**	Nautical mile: 6,076.1 feet (2,025.4 yards)
Lock-on (lock up)	To follow a target automatically in one or more dimensions (e.g. range, bearing, elevation) by means of a radar beam	**NVG**	Night vision goggles
		Orbit	A circular or elliptical pattern flown by aircraft to remain in a specified area
Lt Col	Lieutenant Colonel (LTC in US forces)	**OTH**	Over the horizon
Lt Cdr	Lieutenant Commander	**Overshoot**	To pass through the defender's flight path in the plane of symmetry
LWS	Laser warning system		
M	Mach	**PGM**	Precision guided munitions
Mach	The ratio of an aircraft's velocity to the velocity of sound in surrounding medium	**Pipper**	A 2mm-diameter dot in the centre of the optical sight reticle (gunsight); a dot of light within a lighted ring – used for aiming
Maj	Major		
Maximum power	Afterburner	**Pk**	Probability of kill

Pulling lead	Act of aiming the nose of the aircraft ahead of an enemy aircraft; used primarily in a weapons firing manoeuvre	**Six**	Six o'clock position or area; refers to the rear or aft area of an aircraft
Pylon	A projection under an aircraft's wing, designed for suspending ordnance, fuel tanks or pods	**Skyhawk**	Douglas A-4 (Ahit or Eagle)in Israeli service)
Python	Israeli-built air-to-air missile	**Splash**	Term meaning that destruction of the target had been verified by visual or radar
Radar signature	Characteristics peculiar to different aircraft which are distinguishable when displayed on a radar scope	**Strike**	An attack upon a surface target, intended to inflict damage on or destroy an enemy objective
Recce	Reconnaissance	**S turn**	A turn to one side of a reference heading followed by a turn to the other side; provides a difficult tracking problem for ground radars
Recon	Reconnaissance (US)		
RESCAP	Rescue combat air patrol	**SyAAF**	Syrian Arab Air Force
Reticle	Optical sight reticle; a system of lines around a dot (pipper) in the focus of an optical gunsight that provides a reference for aiming and estimating range and distance to the target	**TAC**	Tactical Air Command
		TAC	Tactical
		Tacair	Tactical air
		Tally-ho	Term meaning that the target has been visually sighted
RHAW	Radar homing and warning; onboard aircraft equipment to warn pilot of active enemy defences	**TFS**	Tactical Fighter Squadron
		TFW	Tactical Fighter Wing
Ripple fire	Rapid sequential firing of two or more missiles	**Tomcat**	Grumman F-14 carrier-based fighter
RTB	Return to base	**TOT**	Time over target
Ra'am	F-15I (Thunder) in Israeli service	**Tracking**	Term referring to the maintaining of the centre of the field of view of search radars or airborne sensors on a target
RAF	Royal Air Force		
RNLAF	Royal Netherlands Air Force		
RWR	Radar warning receiver	**Unk**	Unknown
SAM	Surface-to-air missile	**US**	United States (of America)
SA-2	Soviet surface-to-air missile (NATO codename Guideline)	**USAF**	United States Air Force
		USMC	United States Marine Corps
SA-6	Soviet mobile surface-to-air missile (NATO codename Gainful)	**USN**	United States Navy
		USSR	Union of Soviet Socialist Republics
Shafrir	Israeli air-to-air missile	**UAV**	Unmanned Aerial Vehicle

Vector	A command which directs an aircraft to follow a specific heading
VFR	Visual flight rules
VID	Visual identification
Weapons system	Refers to the combination of aircraft, crew ordnance, avionics, etc.
Winchester	Term indicating that all ordnance has been expended
Wingman	Pilot (or aircraft) that flies at the side and to the rear of an element leader. In an aircraft flight, 02 is wingman to lead (01), and 04 is wingman to 03. Usually, more experienced pilots fly lead and 03 positions in a flight, and these pilots initiate combat actions while their wingmen fly cover
WMD	Weapons of Mass Destruction
WSO	Weapons System Officer
WVR	Within visual range
Zoom	An unloaded climb used to gain maximum altitude whilst dissipating minimum energy